**Truth and Heresy on Bobby's Camino**

**By Bobby Morrell**

**ISBN:** 9798324166779

Disclaimer: This is a work of memory, for any mistakes or errors I apologise unreservedly.

©R Morrell 2024

Contents:

| | |
|---|---|
| The Prologue | Page 7 |
| Camino Frances Map | Page 10 |
| Chapter 1 Home to St Jean Pied de Port, France. | Page 11 |
| Chapter 2. St Jean Pied de Port to Zubiri. | Page 23 |
| Chapter 3. Zubiri to Najera | Page 45 |
| Chapter 4. Najera to Burgos | Page 65 |
| Chapter 5. Burgos to Sahagun | Page 88 |
| Chapter 6. Sahagun to Leon | Page 114 |
| Chapter 7. Leon to Foncebadon | Page 135 |
| Chapter 8. Foncebadon to Villafranca | Page 170 |
| Chapter 9. Villafranca to Sarria | Page 198 |
| Chapter 10. Sarria to San Xulain | Page 234 |
| Chapter 11. San Xulian to Santiago | Page 261 |
| Chapter 12. Santiago to Home | Page 299 |
| Afterword | Page 324 |

Authors Note: If you are planning to walk the Camino de Santiago for reasons of faith then this book is probably not for you. If you are planning to walk it for other reasons, then this book will give you an honest appraisal of my experience walking the Camino Frances in August-September 2023. This book is in no way a travel guide, there are plenty of those. It is, I hope, an account of a typical pilgrim and it is designed to help past, current and new pilgrims to understand something of the strange road to Santiago, that continues to fascinate, a thousand years on.

I thought it may also be the story of a romantic fool, or as someone said, a deluded idiot. I think they're the same thing, aren't they?

Each chapter features a selection from my Bob's Camino Playlist – on Spotify, and one of my Sonnets, written on the Camino.

**The Prologue**

Through August and September 2023, I walked 500 miles from the south of France, over the Pyrenees across the north of Spain on the ancient pilgrim route, the Camino de Santiago. Many thousands make this journey every year, and this was a life experience I had been thinking about for over twenty years and planning for a year. My life had changed significantly in the previous 12 months, and I needed to do something to draw a line under certain parts, and also to deal with, and throw off, if possible, some of the elements that were getting in the way of me, getting on with, my life. In this book I will take you through the pre-amble, the initial hard stages, the thought processes, and what they did for me, and lastly, and probably more importantly, the people. The people I met through the walk, from all over the world, and who accepted me, mostly, into their lives for a short time.

As pilgrims there is largely a familial spirit that binds you. You are, after all, attempting the same physical task, which means you have a shared goal. You will all choose different ways, timings, and accommodation options, but in the end, you're all heading the same way, enduring the same mountains and the same weather, the same hard going under foot, and also allowing your brain to try and make sense of the walk, the past, the present and the future, all at once.

As I sit here, remembering so much, there are faces that I immediately remember and miss. These are strangers, and you come to love them, almost immediately. I have to thank, with huge feelings of gratitude, Huw, Tricia, Bonnie, Nicole, Matthias, AJ, Ady, Oka, Marie, Brooke, Cathy, Jane, Jim, Beth, Woody, Nico, Kylie, Emanuele, Matt 1, Matt 2 and Lizzie, Alisha, Alec, Dawn, Jasser, the 3 Stooges, and everyone else. Friends helped me along the way by sending music for Bob's Camino playlist (on Spotify), and through messages of support. They are Emma, Harry and Charlie, Tim and Hayley, Sue, Mariel & Rouven, Sam, Frankie, Marcus, Xander, Lizzie and Oliver, Hannah, Derek, Geoff, Holly, Stacey, Donna, Jo, Tina, Simon, Kirsten, Lorraine, dear Ann, and my closest and dearest friend, Jeremy.

Some of these Pilgrims helped me in ways they will never know. All helped me appreciate the very best of humanity. I miss them, the routine, the walk, the road, the peace, the music, the relationship that grew between my brain, my legs and feet, and the experience. I miss the strange road to Santiago.

Hungershall Park, Tunbridge Wells, Kent, October 2023

The Route Frances from St Jean Pied de Port in France to Santiago de Compostela in Galicia, in Spain.

## Chapter 1 Home to St Jean Pied de Port, France.

*Bob's Camino Playlist Song: Victims by Culture Club*

*'The victims we know so well*
*They shine in your eyes*
*When they kiss and tell*
*Strange places we never see*
*But you're always there*
*Like a ghost in my dreams*
*And I keep on telling you*
*Please don't do the things you do*
*When you do those things*
*Pull my puppet strings*
*I have that strangest void for you'*

**Sonnet 1** *(Pre Camino)*
And the path calls me, dragging me, onward
Not then, but now, today, away from this
To a place of peace where I can't be reached
To somewhere I am unknown, of silence.
I walk there steadily away from you
(Where I don't have to await the sure fear,
Where I won't fight demons attacking you,
Assaulting our thoughts and bodies in here,
In the mind, where tricks and the past haunt you
Where lies and truth don't exist any more
Where Chaos triggers hated self-conflict
Where, like a locked door, life is surely closed)
Each pace eases my pain, then doubles it,
Till the end where neither of us will be.

What is the Camino? The Camino de Santiago de Compostela (The Way of St James – the Compostela is the pilgrims proof that they have made the walk) is a pilgrimage, a long walk. For a millennia, millions have walked away from their homes, all across Europe, and then more recently, from anywhere in the World, to find their way to this small Spanish city where, supposedly, an Apostle is entombed. There are many routes to Santiago (Saint James) in Spain, and the main one, the traditional route, is over 500 miles across the Iberian peninsula. I was making this pilgrimage so I could escape from my life for a while. This is a story of the heart.

It had been a long, rough year. Since lockdown, I had struggled with a deep depression, and my relationship with my wife had suffered as a result. Ultimately, I became involved in a torrid and unforgiveable love affair, which culminated in me leaving my family home, and moving into my own place, only to then have my heart broken, and I became even more depressed. Of course, there's much more to this story, but that's for another time.

I accept my own part in this myriad of sins. I take responsibility as far as I can. I have suffered and accepted the emotional punishment due to me. There were times, when I sat in my cottage, where I was plunged into the very depths of despair and nothing is worth that. You ignore the warnings, because you are a deluded fool. There are choices you make, that you sense will end badly, and yet you make them anyway, because you are a fool, hoping your version will be different. You know that in other's eyes, you will never be forgiven, and this is a hard thing to accept, that someone will hate a part of you forever. You also realise that in order for you to function, once it all falls apart, you must, in some way, be able to let go, and forgive yourself. Even if it's just a notional feeling, it's important, if you aren't to live your life wallowing in the pain. As I say, though, I was a fool. I must and will, always deeply regret what happened, and the way it happened.

Early on, I had decided that if I was ever to walk the Camino, the full one from France to Santiago, then this would be the year and I had booked the time off from work. Through the year, as this hellish period unfolded, I quietly prepared for this trip. I went on a few shortish hikes, I went on two longer ones around a local lake, I walked around my town which has fabulous circular walks interspersed by occasional pubs. I was trying to prepare for 20 plus kilometres every day. I had no idea how long it would take – maybe five, maybe seven weeks, so my leave was open ended. The preparation, such as it was, was one of the few things that kept me on an even keel. Without the walking, from my little house, into the countryside that was on my doorstep, life would have been impossible.

Over the previous twelve months I had mourned the end of my marriage. I had grieved for it. Knowing my own actions had rendered it over and that the pain I had caused was unfairly dealt out to people who truly didn't deserve it.

I had also got used to living alone, I spent long weekends alone and feeling lonely. I came to understand loneliness. I had never been properly alone before, and I had not expected to be alone now. To make matters worse, it was a loneliness I had brought on myself. I was also taking anti-depressants but was aware that I didn't want to stay on them. I managed to come off them completely before the walk, but during that awful year, there were times when they were essential.

I had been out with several women from dating apps or through introductions. There was the midget, the nun, and the nympho. The midget was a mistake, the nun was pretty galling (vow of chastity, I kid you not) and the nympho, which sounds like fun, is fine in the short term, but not a long runner, realistically. So, all of these were non-starters. There were a couple of fleeting flings which were fun, and good, for a short time, for my fragile ego. None of this gave me anything like what I needed. I wanted love, pure and simple and my brain could not get past the thought that the love I had pursued, had pulled the rug on me. She is a reappearing character in this comedy. She comes and goes even when I was miles along the Camino. When she appears, we'll call her K. Whilst our relationship was surely over, we maintained occasional contact, as a slightly co-dependent habit we couldn't kick. She was one of the reasons I was walking. To get over what had happened, to get over her. To learn something about myself and to find the courage to move on with my life, with it forever changed. In truth, I was running away from life, and I was also terrified of what I would find there, on this strange road that I was going to take. This was a big step.

When I arrived in St Jean Pied de Port, in Southern France I was in a highly emotional state. The effort to get away and to get there, the start of the walk, was huge. I took a train in and out of London to Gatwick Airport, stayed in a pod-based hotel for a few hours then flew to Bilbao. In Bilbao I had my haircut very short by a chap who had no English at all. I learnt that 'un poco fuera de la cima' means 'a little bit off the top'. Then a hot, four-hour bus ride to Bayonne in France. Then a run across from the bus stop to the station for the train to St Jean. It was a killer of a day. When I got off the train I was determined to get to the pilgrims office to get my Compostela – the form you needed to collect stamps from hostels along the road, and to register as a pilgrim. I walked purposefully up the hill and got more and more emotional. As I arrived, I fell into the building almost unable to speak. A nice chap calmed me down. I felt so moved, I couldn't breathe. 'It's taken me so long to get here' I said. And I didn't just mean that day. I meant my whole life. So long to be able to step away from existence for something personal and challenging. So long to be able to turn up and defy my own instincts and know that I would walk 500 miles across the top of Spain in the next 5 weeks or so. At this point the 500 miles seemed the least of my concerns. It had taken everything just to get to St Jean. It was also much more than that. It was also 'it has taken me so *much* to get here.' This was the very start of my healing and the journey there, had been like breaking off an infected limb to try and stop the infection of sadness spreading everywhere.

I was lucky enough to get Duc. He was gentle with me, and slowly talked me through the route, the journey, the ups and downs. They know that day one is by far the worst, and I suppose they want to make sure you get through that and not pull out. I was, as you know, walking this for personal reasons. The emotion swept over me, coupled with fear that I was not ready for this, in any way. Fear of the huge mountain staring down at me, which I would be walking up the next day.

Let's look at the facts. In the United Kingdom there's a thing called the 3 Peaks Challenge. In 24 hours you walk up and down Mount Snowdon in Wales, Scafell Pike in England, and Ben Nevis in Scotland. Snowdon is 1,085 metres, Ben Nevis is 1,345 metres and Scafell is a paltry 978 metres. I know people who have done the 3 peaks, and there's no question that it's doable, but it is also a risky thing to do. Sometimes people get into trouble and I would imagine the mountain rescue people must be pretty sick of it. Day 1 of the Camino, starting in St Jean Pied de Port (the port of the feet, literally), takes you up to 1,427 metres, and then down at least 650 metres the other side, which is a killer. The way up is extremely steep. You are carrying 10 kilos minimum on your back too, and almost certainly you aren't carrying enough water. Few are ready for this, and many break the climb after about 12km at the Albergue (pilgrims hostel) at Orisson.

**St Jean Pied de Port Station before breaking down!**

**Duc in the Pilgrim Office (thanks for the photo Jim.)**

## Chapter 2. St Jean Pied de Port to Zubiri.

*Bob's Camino Playlist Song: Ramble on by Led Zeppelin.*

'Ramble on
And now's the time, the time is now
To sing my song
I'm goin' 'round the world, I got to find my girl
On my way
I've been this way ten years to the day
I gotta Ramble on
Gotta find the queen of all my dreams'

## Sonnet 2: Sounds of the Camino
In the dorm there are hours of dark noises
Muffled movement and the clang of alarms
Then the hoarse gasps over hard, steep inclines
And in the half-light, real long silences.
The mountain bells signal the pastoral
The cries of the eagles waiting for prey
Above the distant river, calling us
From the tap of our sticks, feeling our way.
The snores are masked by the monk's sad vespers,
Tolling the bells for our primal emotions
As the wind shocks our souls and sparks resets
Every story true, set on punishment,
All the reasons and none, bring us to here
All the sounds send away, for now, our fear.

**The moment of departure – quite terrifying.**

On any day, this walk is hard. The day I left, on the 19th August, within a few hours, I was walking in a punishing 30 degree plus heat. I hadn't slept much. I'd had a light meal, and shower, then I tried to catch a few hours in my first Albergue, at the top of the hill, beyond the pilgrims office in St Jean. I was in a room with 4 others. They all snored. I imagine I did too, and lights out is 10pm so I definitely slept for a few hours. At about 4.30am people start moving around, and eventually at about 5.15 I was up and getting ready. It was pitch black outside. The hostel offered free instant coffee and toast and jam for breakfast. I was to find out that this was rare. I had a quick coffee and some bread, but I wasn't hungry. I was aware that every minute was delaying the start of over 25km up and over this mountain, and that if I didn't start, then I was risking not making it at all. Irrationally, you imagine having to sleep rough on the mountain, being attacked by bears or wolves (highly unlikely) or dying of thirst or hunger. (I've since learned that there are both bears and wolves in parts of Spain, I was unaware of this throughout the walk!).

I managed to strap my weighty pack on and set off down through St. Jean. The cobbled streets, with the yellow arrows, and the shell-shaped signs show you the way. I had an elasticated torch on my forehead which blinds anyone you speak too, immediately. I felt like an explorer striking out into unknown territory on my own. I assumed there would be a bed for me in the monastery over the mountain, but I didn't know for sure, so this was a first too, the beginning of a daily uncertainty that many could not cope with. Millions had done this same thing before, but for me, for each new pilgrim, you realise that this is what you are here to do, and for you, it feels like you are a pioneering soul.

I met a young Dutch chap called Jasser, and we started a conversation. I was again, very emotional. He was on a career break, at 28, working out what he wanted to really do with his life. I envied him the choice. I envied him his youth. When he asked me why I was doing this, I tried to give him an answer, but it was so hard. To get over something. To get over someone. To move on, to forgive, or just say something romantic like 'for reasons of the heart.' It's not that romantic, it feels a bit pathetic. We walked the first 10km or so together. It started to get steep almost immediately. So, you are leaning forward, with a heavy weight on your back, puffing along up a rapidly warming hill, that is practically vertical. For a little while I thought he and I were walking at a similar pace. He suddenly looked up another hillside and just said 'I'm going to speed up, I'll see you later' – and he was gone! This was pretty demoralising, as I was just managing to keep up with him. Just before Orisson it's really steep, and rocky and hard. I didn't have a stick to keep me upright, or to lean on, so I was dependent on my own strength to keep me from falling. Within minutes I was sweating buckets, couldn't get enough water regardless of how many swigs I took, and was breathing like a wheezing heavy smoker. I was cursing my lack of preparation and wondering if I was going to make it over the mountain at all. I was surrounded by mountain sheep with their clanging bells, misty views down into France, which were stunning, and these paled a bit when feeling so utterly puffed-out.

When I saw Orisson, it was incredible. It's the most beautiful Albergue with a large terrace, like a Ski hotel, and a stunning view. I had coffee, pastry and bought a banana. And I was lulled into a massive false sense of security. I thought, 'If there's places like this every few miles then this is going to be fine! Of course! Of course, they will use it to make money, so they will have calculated that every few miles people will pay serious money for refreshment!' Oh, how wrong can you be?

**Orisson: Being lulled into a false sense of security**

I carried on up the hill and because of its steepness you go slowly. Every step is hard, every step you are breathing heavily, every step you wonder how many you need to take before the next swig of water. The views are amazing. At certain points you look ahead and the road winds up into the mountain and you think, that must be near the top? It isn't. So, you stop for brief breaks. But you also know that every minute you are resting going up, adds another to getting across the top and then down the other side, which means a minute hotter than before and you are piling exhaustion on sweaty exhaustion.

Other pilgrims pass you. They say 'Bon Camino' which is the cry of the entire walk, or 'Buen Camino' in Spain, sometimes. This is nice. At this point on Day 1 many other questions come from this. How are they able to be passing me? How unfit am I if these people are flying up this hill? This hill that is higher than Ben Nevis? Am I going to die here on this mountainside and will countless pilgrims pass my rotting corpse and point out the fate that awaits unprepared pilgrims? Near Orisson I spotted an attractive French lady in an orange top going at roughly a similar pace to me. She avoided any eye contact and we didn't speak. Even so we mirrored each other up this damned mountainside. She even had a ciggie at Orisson. I thought wow, she's that fit and a smoker! Couple of times I smiled as she passed and she ignored me. Fair enough. She was probably terrified I'd keel over and she'd have to administer mouth to mouth. We'll come back to her.

The road snaked up the pass, there were occasional cars and bikes that went by, and some pilgrims had really cool gear. Mine was okay I thought, although my blue cargo shorts were already heavy with sweat around my hairy arse. Music helped. 'Ramble on' by Led Zeppelin was really motivational and you found yourself walking to the beat of each song, which in many cases was helpful. Some of the sadder songs had additional resonance. You felt you were mounting this hillside as a form of punishment for the heartbreak you had caused and part of you thought you were, somehow, deserving of this torture.

As I approached the summit, the sun high in the sky now, there was a white van dispensing refreshment. The rotund and grinning Frenchman who runs it, is a cynic. He sells water, beer, food etc. As you stand there, dying, covered in sweat, he shows you a crude design on the side of his van. 1km up, 5km over, then 5km down. Put like that it looks doable. It is a lie. It's there to wind you up a few kilometres later, knowing that you can't go back and smack him one. The 1km up is right. It's such a hard 1000 metres. Very steep and you are heading for a small gap in the mountain, the pass that takes you into Spain. When you reach it, which takes forever, you feel ready to hail a cab. You walk straight for a few metres, essentially across the border, but the romance of this is lost, trust me. Then you see a copper-coloured tap dispensing water. You consume gallons of ice-cold water and I swear it never tasted so good. It's now lunchtime and you've been walking over 6 hours and think you're going to die. A little after this I ran into the orange-topped lady again. This time she looked as knackered as me and was sitting under a tree. Now she spoke. The shared exhaustion of this moment united us. Momentarily, I thought, I can stand the thought of running into you along the next 500 miles, but then – no. She had walked from Carcassonne on the French way and was stopping at Roncesvalles – the next hostel. Her last, my first. She admitted this day was the hardest. This was the pinnacle and finale of our brief encounter. Still, we had gone from strangers to acquaintances in a few short, hot hours.

So, now I was walking relatively straight across, as the white van had promised. There was the sound of mountain rivers below, sheep clanging along, massive birds of prey circling overhead (probably vultures waiting for me to expire) stunning views of Spain in the distance and an anticipation of the downward trajectory, which I was longing for. Then the white van man's sense of humour was revealed. It wasn't 5km across, it was a few km across and then another 3 or 4 straight up! I sat for a while by a disused building looking at the view and wondering when my body would be found if I just died here. A Frenchman called Charlie stopped for a chat. He explained he had sent his rucksack on by car (it costs 6 euros per day to do this – I never did) and that there was no shame in it. He was a cheerful soul.

The next few kilometres, in the heat of the day, are very hard, because you thought it was going to be flat, and it's not. And you're in pain as you go along, and you're tired and exhausted. Also at this height, the air is thinner, so you are breathing like an ox. Eventually, you see a sign sending people down, and many, like me, take the wrong path. One path leads you down a gentle meandering roadway to the monastery. The other, the wrong one, leads you straight down a vertical path that reverses the efforts your legs have been through and now introduces you to pushing your feet with all your weight (overweight in my case) into the toes of your boot for 2 hours. Your shins start smarting immediately and you tell yourself it's only a few kilometres when it's feeling like a downward-only marathon. Every turn you think, I must be nearly there now, but you're not. My breathing became so laboured and loud, like a horn, almost every breath, I really sensed the end was near. When, quite suddenly, it evens out, you cross a bridge and there is the building. It's a very large, pale multi-windowed affair with a double door. I fell into it and a lovely attendant got me water, and helped me to check in. I felt like I must have looked like someone in acute need of an ambulance. In ten minutes, I was standing under a shower. I stood there for 40 minutes. I had bitten off more than I could chew. I was hopelessly unprepared and another day like this was sure to end my life. I seriously considered ending my walk right there and getting a train to Barcelona and hiding there for a few weeks, but I couldn't stand the shame of returning without, at least, trying to complete this impossible task. The shower gave me life. I napped for a little, and then went in search of dinner in a local restaurant. Next to me, in the hostel was Oka, a red-haired dutchman. He was friends with a man I'd seen on the road who was carrying an immense pack, whom I had labelled The Kurgan after the baddie in *Highlander*. He was a bald man who looked supremely fit, but was struggling all day up the mountain, and looked like he was slightly deranged. Oka was a really nice guy and we met a few times after that, with his 2 Stooges (the Kurgan and Hamidi from Morocco who was painfully thin and smoked like a chimney.)

Dinner was with Jasser (who looked surprised I had made it – so was I) and two other chaps. Dinner was 3 courses and wine – not bad for 12 euros. I had a couple of cold beers which were required, and I sat on a terrace feeling like a tourist. I also sat on a bench and felt my joints beginning to seize. I then hobbled back to the monastery. I had bought some cheap sandals for the evenings, but they weren't cushioned much and so after the day in my boots, these meant you were hobbling around. I slept well.

At 6am we were woken by the monks in the monastery singing vespers. The chanting was, I suppose, vaguely tuneful but my body felt like it had been wrenched through a medieval racking torture and my feet felt like they had been hammered by a mallet. I looked across at Oka and we agreed that what the monks were singing was 'please get up and fuck off!' so we did.

The single relief is that you know that this day you have just survived is the worst. There are more tough mountains ahead, but this one prepares you for them, because they may be higher, but they won't be as hard. As you leave the hostel the next morning you see a sign saying 'Santiago de Compostela 790' which is slightly depressing. It looks like a long way. It really is. After about 5km there are cafes where you can buy coffee which brings you to life and makes you feel more civilised. You know it's only two days to Pamplona the first city. On the app and the maps it doesn't look that far. At one point I was passed by two local Spanish people walking on the path, but clearly they weren't pilgrims because they had no stuff. 'Where are your rucksacks?' I joked. The man came straight back with 'Two children, that's my rucksack!" Pretty good come back I thought.

**The famous sign outside Roncesvalles**

The walk to Zubiri was lots of different terrain including roadside walking and steep hills.

Zubiri is a small village really with a good bar selling cold beer and pork strips – at least that's what they looked like. After a night there in a slightly different style of hostel, purpose built but small, I woke from a deep sleep to find most people had left. The walk down to Zubiri is more pleasant that the Day 1. Each small incline feels like a challenge but you know that the trend is down or straight so it's okay. The rivers are still there accompanying you along, there are nice pilgrims passing and waiting in different places and you sense you are part of this line of humanity stretched out across the hillsides. You are of course, in Basque country, which spans the Pyrenees and you are now in the machine that is the 20-25km set recommended walking day, if you want to make it to Santiago in a reasonable time period.

Those first few days through Zubiri and into Pamplona and a little beyond served as a challenging and boiling hot introduction to the walk, but also a re-acquaintance with myself. I found myself becoming very angry. As if I was waking up from a terrible dream or a magic spell which had forced me to become someone that I wasn't. All of my fellow pilgrims, seemed like really nice people. I was sensing that they would see through my exterior and expose what I had become, or rather, what I saw myself as. I was down on myself, didn't like myself, in truth I didn't really know myself. I had spent so long in various forms of depression, unhappiness, over-compensation, avoidance mode, self-loathing and was also now broken hearted, that I imagined that it seeped out of me to anyone I came near. But here people were polite. They said 'hello', 'Bon Camino' and one day, when limping along, a big moustached Frenchman grabbed me by my shoulders and encouraged me. Where did that come from? I was so unused to this level of kindness.

Very quickly I started to go through the emotional turmoil of the previous 12 months. I was so sad for my family, my wife, myself. Sad for K, but I also felt angry that because of what had happened between us, I now disliked myself even more. Again, I must take responsibility for my words and actions, after all, no one makes you do anything, but I did feel angry towards her. I told her this on one of the days when she called me. She wasn't happy hearing it and I'm sorry, but it needed to be said.

The truth was that the act of intense walking and the exertion coupled with the time to think, had shaken me into realising some stuff I had avoided or just not seen. For the first time in months, I felt like I was disconnecting from this situation and was emotionally healing from the months of pain.

I repeatedly became upset when I thought of every individual person who was directly affected by my actions. I could have and should have handled it better with more honesty. I know that some may never forgive me, which I will have to learn to live with. I regret causing that pain to my very soul.

As well as all those personal agonies, I was also starting to figure out what the hell I was going to do with the rest of my life, now that all of my previous plans and dreams had been abandoned. What if I never met anyone else? What if I could never love again? All of this was running through my brain in those early days, and there is something in this process of emotional self-flagellation that also triggers other ridiculous and utterly deluded daydreams. Where you believe that proof of your contention that this journey is right for you, will arrive in the form of a new holiday romance. For an ego like mine that's a constant thought and you can guess where this is going. I was looking for a validator, a saviour if you will, to bestow some miraculous cure for all of my ills. In the first days, before you've formed friendships you look around suspecting that this crowd will even out, and you'll find someone to be your companion for weeks. When you don't see a potential romance in their ranks then your mind starts to look for one. What a total waste of thought.

**Chapter 3. Zubiri to Najera**

*Bob's Camino Playlist Song: The Man in Me by Bob Dylan*

'The man in me will do,
Nearly any task,
And as for compensation ,
There's a little he would ask
It takes a woman like you
To get through, to the man in me.'

**Sonnet 3: Tilting at Women**

She looks nice, just my type, amazing eyes
Petit figure, vulnerable, been hurt,
Challenging, out of my league, eye contact
She's talking to me, that's it, she's mine.
Maybe she's the one, no chance, but she's talking
I'm her romance, her knight, her saviour,
She's being kind, stop confusing false looks,
Inventing a life that is yours, never.
You are not twenty-five, your time is past,
Leave them to heaven, youth and Javier
You cannot fix their disinterested hearts,
You're just an acquaintance of a few days,
What a sad idiot that she's seen through
Give it up, you stupid, romantic fool.


When we approached the first big city, Pamplona, you

cross a bridge (there is generally a bridge) and you can see

the spread of the city in front of you. What you don't

realise is that it's another 8 km to the hostel in the centre. This is a feature of some of the other cities too, where you have to walk along concrete streets for miles to get to the centre which is a pain because they are like any other city on Earth, very dull, and if you knew in advance then you'd take a bus. Which from then on, many of us did. This day I stopped at a small chapel with Carmella? from Italy and was delighted to think I was nearly in the centre. Hours later I was cursing, still trying to find the gate in the walls to get into the city centre. A lovely lady in the hostel did my washing for me and I sat in a bar for a couple of hours drinking beer and feeling a little lonely, and then ate alone that evening, which was a meal of delicious lamb chops, but again, lonely. That evening I got chatting to an Italian guy from Veneto who I'd seen a few times on the road. He was Massimo, a butcher I think, and we went to the famous bar where Hemingway used to drink and took pictures with the bronze statue. Massimo was walking to a strict timetable knowing when he needed to get his flight home, and soon after I didn't see him again. Maybe it was me! I liked Pamplona but felt no compulsion to stay here for longer than one night.

**Massimo, Me and Ernest.**

    I then made it back to the hostel for lights out. In the big dorm it was very hot indeed and I came out at 3am to the reception area where there was a fan, and me and an Australian girl called AJ, lay on the couches and tried to remain cool. Hours later you're up, it's still dark and you're getting ready to leave.

It was at this point that I spotted the most gorgeous, elfin woman. She was unusual because she was petite, very slim and had white beads all over her head which gave her a look like a sort of, hippie dancer. She was getting ready to walk and she was also talking to others including a bloke and I assumed they were an item. Of course, someone as lovely as that would surely be with someone. However, she was the first woman I had seen so far that properly turned my head. We all left Pamplona in the pitch dark and made our way out through a large park which I promptly got lost in which delayed me by at least thirty minutes. Once I was on the right road it was a shlep out of the city via another café, where I bought breakfast for a sweet student from Oxford, and then on. As you leave Pamplona behind, you scale another mountain, not that high actually, but high enough when it's hot, and this used to be called the Mountain of Forgiveness. It's quite odd to walk across the place when you really feel like you would either like some forgiveness from someone, or that you are owed some, or that you must forgive yourself. The route up is quite gentle. There are metal pilgrim statues at the top and everyone stops for photos. I was relieved that the 'Mountain' was nothing compared to the Pyrenees. I had heard about this place in the audiobook of *The Pilgrimage* by Paulo Coelho. Forgiveness is a really tough concept and I must say, apart from the relief of getting to the plateau I didn't feel in any way forgiven, or that I could very well forgive myself. The route down is steep and very rocky with loose stones everywhere. There are man-made platforms covered in rock that gently bring you down, but it's fast and in my case almost deadly. My blisters were getting much worse and I was favouring my right foot because my left was so painful. On one of these platforms I tripped on a rock, fell from the highest point, and managed to twist at the last moment so I finished on my pack. It still hurt. I managed to get back up, and this fall shook me. An injury like a sprain, or worse a fracture, would be the end of everything. I realised I would need a stick. Right now though, it was so hot I was slowly walking between shady trees and bushes. It was on this leg that I met Matthias, a twenty-five year old fisherman from Belgium. He won't mind me saying I am sure, that he was a little overweight and struggling as I was. He went on ahead and we would meet a few more times before splitting at Fromista. Happily we are still in touch. By all accounts he has found romance on the Camino, and I am so happy for him.

    The next stop was a lovely town called Puenta de la Reina where there is a beautiful bridge, ancient too, over a large river. My feet by now, were agony. After checking in and showering at a hostel I went to the Pharmacia where a charming girl sold me Compeed blister plasters and a pair of cushioned insoles for my boots, plus proper EU strength Ibuprofen tablets, 400mg each. I wouldn't use these until the next day so had a quiet evening hobbling around the area of town I was in and drinking a couple of beers. I remember calling Ann, my friend and colleague, and it was so good to hear her voice as I gently danced around the bridge. That night at dinner I met Matt and Lizzie, he was ex US Army and hyper friendly, and she was very smiley. He had done this before so was used to it all. We chatted and they were sweet, and we were all in the same hostel. As we made it back to the rooms it became clear that our rooms were like saunas – it was over 26 degrees outside at 11 o'clock at night, way too hot to be in an enclosed room that was even hotter. I brought out my sleeping roll onto the terrace and lay it down under the stars and slept for at least 2 hours. Everyone else was on chairs or lying on tables. The lady who ran the place suddenly appeared and was embarrassed by seeing everyone strewn across the terrace. I was in my underpants, and I think, hanging out of them when she woke us, for which I must apologise. She helped us bring all of our mattresses out on to the terrace and there we all slept. I slept next to Lizzie, really odd I suppose after meeting her a few hours before. No one cared, it was too hot. This is the first time I have slept under the stars for years, if not perhaps the first time. If it wasn't for the agony in my feet it would have been lovely. By six the next morning I was in my new padded boots, had taken my pills and was on the road, in the dark, crossing the Puenta and making my way towards Estella. The pills made the walk in the morning bearable. But you knew that each step was attacking your feet and the pills were masking the damage you were doing to them. I took one picture of my right foot and it looked like I'd been tortured.

**The Bridge at Puenta De La Reina – I've spared you the pic of my foot!**

I think this may have been the day where I first met her. I was walking on my own at a pretty slow pace and amazingly as she passed, with a group of people, our eyes met. This was a definite moment. She was probably thinking, hmm, another pilgrim with sore feet. I was thinking, wow she actually looked at me, maybe she's the one! Christ, what a fool.

I stopped at a café and she was there too and said hello to me, and I smiled and said hello back. That was it. What made her talk to me? Desire? Of course not, she was just being polite and friendly. I, unreasonably, thought this was possibly the start of some walking romance. The walk that day was long and very hot to a town called Estella, and amazingly, as I approached it, soon to pass over yet another bridge, there she was coming in the other direction. She said hello, she was staying at an Albergue I had just passed on the outskirts. We got talking, her English was excellent, she was from Malaga and her name was Marienma, a name I had never heard before. She was humming and haring about whether to complete the

Camino on this trip. I became stupidly emotional and tried to explain how I had come to be there. She asked me if I was a coach which I am, and we, I thought, connected a little. I was over the moon. We parted and I felt that there was almost certainly something going on here. What a totally hopeless romantic fool. Anyway, I made it into town, had a couple of beers and a tortilla to celebrate and stayed in a private room in a hostel with a fan which was amazing, and which meant I actually got some sleep. I ate in an air-conditioned restaurant and tried to get an early night, whilst tending to my poor feet. I should explain that I stayed in occasional hotels or private rooms in hostels which cost a little more. This was actually essential because the sleep wasn't the best in the Albergue and once in a while you needed peace and your own space.

    The next day at dawn I was up and out again, more pain killers taken and up onto the road. This was a really hard day all the way to Los Arcos. This was probably one of the hottest days, across fields with very little cover or shade. Each day I would listen to my music, after some peace. There were stunning sunrises, and varying views, and small villages that sometimes had open cafes and some that did not. My mother had lent me a baseball cap which actually saved my life. You wore it at an angle so the sun was kept off your face, and at times, the thirst was unquenchable. After about 15 km, in a field, there was a van run by two lovely ladies dispensing drinks. I bought water and Kas Naranja from them and sat for a while. It was another 6km or so to the destination town, which seemed okay, once you'd drunk something. I knew if I didn't leave soon I never would. My feet were throbbing, I was drenched in sweat and my pack seemed so heavy. Also, because of the pain, it was taking me a few hundred metres to get into a rhythm. So much so that I would stand, and gently, inexorably move forward and then in time, speed up to more or less a normal pace. One of the ladies must have observed me as I moved away at a snail's pace from the sanctuary of their van, and came running out behind me, 'Signor! Signor! If you can't go on call 116, it is the Guardia Civil and they will come and pick you up and take you to the next town...' I was shocked at this suggestion and also amused 'Do I really look that bad...? – Do I look like I need that?" I was trying to be funny. She waved me away as if to say – it's your funeral – and it nearly was.

That 6km into Los Arcos was exposed and in the high thirties. I drank everything I had after about 3km. I then walked between tiny shrubs that offered millimetres of shade. A Belgian guy joined me, we were in the same boat, agonising feet and dying in the heat, plus he had no English. Eventually, there in the distance was the shade of a large building and it felt like walking through an oven to get to it. It took forever. But when you did, my god, it was a vending café, with machines offering chilled drinks. It must have taken a fortune that day. We sat outside it sipping our drinks as other dying pilgrims came in. Ady turned up who was AJ's boyfriend from Oz, with his brimmed hat and immense boots for his tiny frame, Oka and 2 of the 3 stooges turned up and we relaxed there together with the Belgian, relieved to have some respite. I then made it into an odd hostel where Oka and I shared again, and I went into town to find an air-conditioned bar, and there was one. Whilst I was sitting there enjoying a beer she appeared with her beady braids, walking past, and I waved, and in she came. She was going swimming and offered me to come – I should have done, of course, but my feet were so buggered and I was covered in a rash over my shoulders from carrying my pack all wrong, so the thought of exposing my body to her at this point was a non-starter. What a bloody fool. Whilst we chatted we established that I had once been an actor, and that she was an ex dancer. We had even more in common. In my mind I was already conjuring trips to Malaga where she would dance for me with her mad hippy hair flying around. She said we must have a conversation about this! I was delighted to do that so we said we'd meet in due course and see each other further along the road. When I thought about this, I had made a friend, one I fancied but I sense that she was moving far quicker than I was. So, I had to plan how to somehow keep up. Because, I thought, if she gets a day ahead of me then I'm never going to make it, we won't meet again and I will lose my chance. That evening, I had another uneventful meal, and went back to the hostel which was mercifully cool. The next day from Los Arcos was a long walk into Logrono. It was another killer day, and that day I had also realised that my new blue cargo shorts had a huge rip across the arse. My backside was hanging out of the damned things. I teamed up with Matthias on this day and we got to a town not far from Logrono called Viana. He stayed there after we had a couple of cold beers, I bought new shorts as the hole in mine was now embarrassing, and then I'm sorry to say, I hitched a lift to Logrono. It was only 7km and it was the hottest part of the day and I would never have made it anyway. I checked in and walked into a square and my god, there she was at a café table. She came over and gave me a hug and kiss on the cheek, we talked about meeting later so I gave her my card (gave her my card? What? Are you joking?) and said text me. I had a quiet evening on my own. She didn't text. And I thought, you know what, she probably thinks you are a creep keeping on turning up like this like a limping pain in the arse, so I decided to give it a break. I went shopping in a supermarket for shower gel, and had a meal in an okay restaurant, and then after a few beers, crashed in a noisy dorm where I was joined in the small hours by Oka again. I didn't think that much of Logrono. It was okay. I decided to stop thinking about girls, keep my distance, and not upset her, and just concentrate on my walk, no-one else's.

    The walk out of Logrono is a long one, and I think it was along here that I bought my first walking staff for ten euros. This turned out to be a great investment because it kept me more upright and gave my arms more of a workout too. Then, that day, the walk changed. We were walking to Najera, which is in Rioja. You're moving from Navarra over the hill, and the walk becomes very rocky and overshadowed by olive trees, and then suddenly the valley opens up before you. Vineyards of deep green surrounded by stunning mountains with brooding clouds coming in. It was immense, spectacular, and I wept. I was so stunned at this beauty. It was unexpected. It was raw and real. I felt so small. I felt so lucky to see this place. I knew no photo would ever do it justice. I drank in the view and hoped I would always keep it close to me. As I sit here now I can see the lush greenery and the rolling hills fading upwards to dark grey clouds. It will always be there. That moment that was so much more important and beautiful than anything. A moment of total perspective.

It was along this road I met individual girls, students and single travellers who had congregated to walk together. I can't remember all of their names. One was behind a bush as I walked down a hill. 'What are you doing?' I asked. 'I'm trying to pee but people keep walking by' she said. 'Go into the vineyard' I suggested. 'I don't like to' 'Darling, you won't be the first or the last' I said, and she laughed. We eventually made it into Najera. It was a small town with a large cliff behind. I stayed at an okay hostel in a room that was a bit like a corridor but the beds were okay. I showered and went out for a wander. I had some lunch and drank some delicious Rioja wine which was very cheap. I seem to remember meeting some people, no one of note though and I think here I was realising that I was going to have to get used to being quite lonely. I was also pretty down on myself for being such a schmuck about the poor lady I had pursued and promised to stay away and play it cool from now on. Two people I had run into a great deal were Shelby, from Far East Asia and a friend of hers, a painfully thin chap who moved like a spider – I can't remember his name, and I would see them appear every day or so. She was smiley and very upbeat, very likeable. Sometimes in these towns, if there wasn't a menu del dia then I would grab a burger and a beer and get ready for sleep and an early start although now the weather was thankfully changing, we didn't have to start quite so early.

**Rioja near Najera**

**Chapter 4 Najera to Burgos**

*Bob's Camino Playlist Song: I am a Man of Constant Sorrow*
*by The Soggy Bottom Boys*
*(O Brother, Where Art Thou?)*

'I am a man of constant sorrow
I've seen trouble all my days,
I bid farewell to old Kentucky
The place where I was born and raised,
(The place where he was born and raised)'

**Sonnet 4: The Eagle's Eye**

What does he see, the kite above the way?
He sees the valley floor, the fast river
The pale fields, the drooping, sad sunflowers
The movement below of a broken line
Broken humanity, trotting, pacing,
Tripping, Tap Tapping, every day below
The same direction, the same objective
Looking down at exhausted, sore feet.
He looks for a mouse, a rodent for lunch,
He sees every move, every flash,
Those eyes searching for some new direction
Those souls, wanting friends and solutions
He hangs there commanding his own eye view
We walk on, oblivious to his ridicule.

The walk across Rioja is more dramatic, with occasional cloud bursts, and a cooler atmosphere at last. I walked on, largely alone, to the next town, Santa Domingo De La Calzada. These days were around 20 kilometres. The walking was around 4 kilometres per hour which seems very slow, but sometimes it was quite steep and sometimes you speed up. So, it was around 5 hours of walking, with a break before you got to the next place. When you're mid-walk, the sun is up and you can see the scenery, and you may have your music on, and you may not. And then your mind goes to work.

There's something that happened to you some time ago. Could be massive, or relatively minor, but whatever it was, at the time you would have said something to yourself like 'I can't deal with this at the moment, so I am going to put it to one side in my brain and deal with it later.' That's the type of thing we all say. Then nothing happens for years and without realising, it eats away at you. Now, on this walk you have the time, and you take that thing and start to think about it and process it. So, for example, I can think about the effect of my actions on my family. The full weight of guilt, shame and agony comes down onto your heart and each step emotionally punishes you. You cannot go back and change it. You have to feel the full weight of the guilt which is agonising, I promise you. You walk along and hot tears fall down your face and you hear the conversations, the words, the ones that were said and all the ones that perhaps should have been said, or the ones that will never be said. It is possible, with hours of time, to deal with some of these issues, as far as perhaps, you ever can. Many feel unresolved still, but you have worked on them. This is important as we will see later. I had never really experienced anything like this before. Or if I had it was over thirty years ago before I was fully grown, and couldn't work on these things as now, where I had the mental acuity to do so. Plus, I was also not under the influence of antidepressants anymore which by their nature, inhibit your feelings, so what you feel is 100% you.

This day to Santa Domingo was relatively short and when I arrived there were queues at the hostel. The lady checking everyone in was taking an age with each person and eventually I got in. After a shower I changed to go for some late lunch. It was a Sunday and mid-afternoon. She, the beaded lady was in the same hostel. I saw her on the phone in the stair well as I walked by and said Hi. That was our only interaction. I wandered around the town but it was late and many restaurants were closing. I walked out of the main drag and found a nice place still serving bar snacks so I had some. I drank a couple of beers and felt warmer and happier. There was a pretty waitress serving me from behind the bar. For no reason I can fathom I thought she fancied me and asked her name. Monika. We shook hands. That was it. I went into flights of fancy in my mind about her, that I would send her a post card from the end of the walk and she would come and join me and I would fly to Bilbao and hire cars to drive down to Rioja to see her. Lucky for her and me, I left before I said anything. I was drinking Rioja for 1 euro 40 per glass – this is ridiculously cheap. I tried to explain to a bar man that a glass of this in London would be over ten pounds – I still don't know if he understood.

    I made it back to the hostel and watched some crap on my phone before crashing out. My dorm was full of Korean ladies and I hope my snoring didn't keep them awake. It was another early start and I stopped at a café on the way out for a pastry and coffee before starting out on the 22 km to Belorado, where my walk would change. It was a more rural walk, riverside I seem to remember. It was here in Rioja that I thought about the eagles overhead. What they must have been thinking about from their great heights and what they must have seen. We must have seemed like a snake of movement below them, from first light until dusk every day, regardless of the weather.

At this point I felt that I didn't have anyone special in my life. I felt that I was largely detested by most of the people I knew, and always would be, and that nobody else was in the least bit interested. This was really hard. To be somewhere on your own, with nobody around you, nobody to speak to, not even someone you can share it with who will understand. You speak to yourself in your head and some of it is not so pleasant. The walk, I seem to remember, was up and down through woods, and I was alone for all of it. I wondered if it was going to be like this all the way to Santiago. I wondered if I just stopped and got a bus then who would know, or care? The music

helped, some of it took me back over thirty years.

Forever Chasing Women

When I was nineteen I flew to the United States to chase a girl, whom I had met when back-packing round Europe. We had a romance in the Cote d'Azur. I followed her to the US (where it ended in tears) and spent a month travelling around the east coast from North Carolina to Montreal. I listened to a couple of albums then, that I was listening to now and it struck me that this was the first time I had been away like this, independently, entirely on my own, since then. I knew it was going to be a reset for me, as I was sure it would be for many others. But I also felt there was a connection with that young past, that I needed to be honest about. I came slowly to understand the type of person I was, what some of my ridiculous character defects were, and always had been, and resolved to change them, or at the very least, stop them appearing. I'm still trying.

When I got to Belorado I checked in and went for a beer. I sat in the square and I think there was a couple there I'd seen on the road and we said hello. I think it may have been a Bank Holiday with a family fair on in the square with cheap rides available for kids. It wasn't much of a place. As I passed a bar there was a drunk who was the spit of Johnny Vegas who tried to make friends with me.

I was having the menu del dia in the hostel and it was there I made a friend. I sat opposite a large, bearded man who looked strangely familiar. We got talking – he was Huw from Wales. An actor. I recognised him from the telly. I was once an actor many years ago. And I had been friends with another actor who looked and sounded very much like Huw. I was moved, choked, I don't know how but we just clicked, as mates. He was doing this for charity in the memory of his nephew, a man who had taken his own life. We chatted to two Danish girls that night, I don't know what happened to them because we never saw them again, maybe they had enough and went home?

> Tony
>
> Tony was my best friend. He was also a well-known character actor. He was a man I met in my local pub who became a father figure, who encouraged me to become an actor, who was generous and very funny and enabling. When he died a few years ago, a part of me died too. He was a big beardy man, funny, full of life, and a devil with the ladies. Whenever I hear Shakespeare, or certain poems, or see men laughing at a bar, or see personality win over looks, I think of him. He was someone I would forever miss and I realised that apart from speaking briefly at his funeral, I had not grieved for him properly. I did on this walk.

The next day we both left at similar times, Huw had terrible blisters and was suffering badly with them. When you're walking the Camino though, it's quite rare for people to walk together. There's an acceptance and a need for everyone to walk at their own speed. It's a tough enough ordeal anyway, so having to keep up with someone, or to slow down for someone just doesn't work, so there's an acceptance that you may or may not walk together. On that first day I remember talking to Huw and explaining that I was also a recently trained Samaritan, and if he wanted to share anything with me, I'd be happy to listen. He did, it was emotional, and the Camino proved itself to be a safe place to speak to people about your feelings. We were also a couple of days away from the next big city Burgos, and we were both looking forward to upgrading to hotels for our first day off since we'd left France. By now we had walked hundreds of miles, and our feet were suffering. I could barely look at mine, they were so sore, with gaping, cracked blisters and open wounds seeping blood into my socks at all times. I showered every day and tried to keep them clean but there was nothing you could do about the 18-25km of relentless punishment they were taking every single day.

It was on this walk Huw told me about Jane – dubbed Calamity Jane by him, who was a tiny Australian lady who seems to have a never-ending series of calamities and problems befall her. We will meet her later.

From Belorado it was a varied walk down to a very hilly region that took you up to a high place through forest which was stunning, challenging, and lovely. I really enjoyed this walk despite the pain. The Ibuprofen were working their magic and I was getting used to using a stick which was definitely helping me along the way. Huw had gone on ahead, but we knew we were staying at the same

Albergue the next evening. I walked past a lady selling refreshments for a donation, and who was carving totem poles and other garden sized ornaments from trees she was cutting down. This day, I actually enjoyed the walk more than I had any other so far on this journey. It was rugged, varied, green and not over long. Eventually I arrived at San Juan de Ortega where most people stayed in the large and badly reviewed monastery and we few who had booked, stayed in the most minute Albergue that had two rooms with 4 beds in each, and a small restaurant and bar. We had a nice evening here with different characters, enjoying a few beers and appreciating the rest and the quiet. I don't remember much about the evening except we were joined by some of the American girls from the walk and got to know them a bit. Huw and I shared the room, he snored a bit as did I, I'm sure, and we were both up early the next day, and the bar below was all locked up and they opened as we came down and we managed to get coffee. This was a long walk today all the way into Burgos. But the good news was that someone had warned us that the last 6km or so, was through a large, dull industrial estate and that almost everyone took the bus from where it began into the town, so we knew that if we made it to there, then we'd be okay. We had both booked hotel rooms with baths which we couldn't wait for, and also the idea of a quiet night without snorers or disturbance was very appealing after 12 days of continuous walking. That walk took us through light rain, sun, wind and a heath-like hillside and then down into a series of villages and hamlets where we found refreshment. There was also a monument to people executed in the Spanish Civil War which Huw knew about and I was moved that this terrible war was still remembered here, as we remember our last war (which the Spanish were neutral for).

At this point Huw and I split and he stormed ahead and I took a more sedate pace. I met a couple who said there was a scenic route into Burgos along the river, and that may well exist but we couldn't see where it began so we skirted the large but fairly pointless airport and joined all the other pilgrims who were waiting for the bus. It was here that I ran into the aforementioned Jane, from Australia. A very short woman in her fifties whom I came to know quite well but who became known to many of us as Calamity Jane. Suffice to say she hit me with three or four complaints immediately, about Albergues, the cost of things and various people who had annoyed her. Much more of her later. The bus ride into Burgos was certainly required because, like so many cities, the outskirts were really offensive after so much beauty. Surprisingly, I saw Marienma from the bus walking with an American chap I had seen before, and, god knows why, but I just thought this was very sad. I went across to the hotel, a beautiful four star where I checked in. As I walked through the doorway I was hit by the scented luxurious air of the top end hotel and became almost emotional! Once in my marble lined room I wallowed in a bath for an hour and spent some time working on my sore feet. I napped, then rather than pay 6 euros for a pair of my socks to be washed, I hand washed my t shirts, pants and socks and hung them up in strategic places around the room. Then I pulled on my jeans and went out into the town, and what a town!

I crossed back over the river into a tree lined, traffic free boulevard, which was breath-taking. Then into the maze of streets that led to the most incredible cathedral I've ever seen. I have no faith as such, but this was one, vast, and intricately designed space that from any angle, in any light, always looked beautiful, with endless spires and huge windows. The streets around led from square, to crescent, to pedestrian shopping street to a vast elongated quadrangle with multiple restaurants all basking within the view of that stunning cathedral. I knew that most pilgrims would be in hostels, and I felt a tinge of guilt that I was living in luxury. I ran into Matt and Lizzie who were in an apartment overlooking the cathedral – Matt said, 'Shit dude, don't feel guilty, that's just one of the advantages of walking the Camino with money!'. That's true, and as it turned out, it was essential to keep me positive.

That evening, I met Huw in a restaurant serving traditional Spanish food which was excellent. We talked about many theatrical stories concerning different, famous, mostly drunken actors. This was so much like my conversations with dear old Tony. It felt very warm and comfortable chatting and laughing and enjoying the business of being in a major city. That night I slept like the dead in my dark air-conditioned room.

The next day was my first proper day off since I'd started the walk, twelve days before. This felt really odd. Firstly, I needed to get up in time for my included, vast breakfast, served in a beautiful high room in the centre of the hotel, which was a converted monastery. Then I had a couple of things to do. The first was to walk around the cathedral, and the second was to visit the castle. The Cathedral was as opulent inside as the outside promised. El Cid, the great unifying symbol of medieval Spain, a knight who fought for both Moor and Christian, is buried there. The rest of the cathedral is almost as outrageously gilted and bright as any other of these Catholic edifices are. As incredible as they are, as an atheist I find them difficult to comprehend. You imagine the poverty that must have existed whilst these places were being built, and the altars designed and created. Someone must have felt that this was totally fine, despite the majority of people starving and accepting the status quo, to build something that was connecting everyone with God? I felt the same in other cathedrals, and also years before at St Peter's in Rome. It's one of the reasons that I barely visited any other chapels on the route of the Camino, there were hundreds, because it doesn't impress me I'm afraid. I find it leaves a bad taste in the mouth. So, once I had paid my respects to Cid, I scooted through the rest of it, got my stamp from a sour faced woman to prove I had been there, and then walked up towards the Castle. This was a relatively steep walk, and led me up to a spectacular, panoramic view of the city. The Cathedral dominates the centre, surrounded by its maze of streets and squares, and there are modern quarters beyond and then the mountains are all around, crisscrossed by motorways. This was a beautiful warm day. At this Castle, The Duke of Wellington, during the Peninsular War where we, the Brits, in 1808, were trying to eject the French from Spain, suffered a major defeat. This, for the Iron Duke was a setback. He attempted to lay siege to the fortress but it was so well defended and provisioned that despite causing several breeches in the walls, he was never able to take the fortress by assault which he had managed at other locations and eventually he had to raise the siege and retreat to Portugal which was a damned long way. The bit I like is about the 'Forlorn Hope' which was the first group of men sent through the breech in the wall to try and secure the space beyond the wall, until more men arrived. It was suicidal mission for all of them, but the corporal and the officer who led a 'Forlorn Hope' would be promoted if they survived which meant more money, so there was a reasonable incentive to give it a go. I recited this story in a video message for my business partner.

    Then after ascending the hillside I made it back down to the town where I bought some t-shirts and socks. I also walked along the boulevard of trees and thought about how romantic it was. I was sad not to be there with a lover but to be there entirely alone. It made my solitude so much worse to be somewhere designed for romance and to be a solo visitor. I met a very good-looking Spaniard and his wife. He was walking a small dog and was perfectly dressed in linen with a jumper over his shoulders, and he had long wavy, model style hair. His name was Xavier. He looked like he belonged there, almost like a placed tourist attraction. How I envied them their seeming idyllic existence. I told them so.

    I went back for a nap, and it was there that I wrote a letter for someone that I felt I very much needed to apologise to. I never sent the letter. But there was something cathartic in writing it.

    That second night Huw and I met up again and after a lovely dinner we had a drink in a square that had multi-coloured lighting. We knew we would meet on the road the next day. Which was the start of the Meseta proper, which was a minimum of a week across the plateau. That night I packed everything for an early start, knowing I would eat well before I left, and then depart my 2-day comfort zone, to go back into hot walking, sore feet and for a while, the long, flat, open fields of the Meseta.

**Burgos Cathedral – spectacular.**

**Chapter 5 Burgos to Sahagun**

Bob's Camino Playlist Song: Running Game (Son of A Slave Master) by Prince

*'Don't Come to the Party unless you bring somebody.*
*Somebody that wants to dance*
*Somebody that wants to make sweet romance,*
*(We still got) mad love for ya, even though, really don't know ya'*

**Sonnet 5: Meseta**

The Way takes you straight across, and too straight,
The path on the plateau barely flexes,
Forcing us to think because it's too easy,
The Towns don't contain enough life for us.
And for miles we pass fields that have haircuts,
Bowing sunflowers begging to be chopped,
Bored barmen serve grudging refreshment,
And on we trudge, desperate for a view.
The quiet villages, again startled,
By new pilgrims spending their meagre pence
The birds are the random movement we like
The path is unmoving, just staying straight
It could be a desert, but it is not,
Leading us gamely, just to get across.


I really loved Burgos and was sad to leave it behind. I slept

poorly on that second night, anticipating the next day's

walk and hoping my feet had healed sufficiently. The walk

out takes you along a straight road and through fields. You pass the University, which must be the most wonderful place to go, and through a small park, until eventually you cross over the motorway and make your way into the flatlands. This is the Meseta. It's not entirely flat as we will see, but it's fairly flat. The word means, table, like a plateau. It doesn't feel like that at the time. Huw was behind me I think – even though I left a little late after a vast breakfast to fill me up until I reached the stop at Hornillos. There were several Korean ladies walking that day. They were always so happy and smiley, always said Bon Camino, and that, sadly was the limit of their conversation. I regret not pursuing those conversations – Huw did and always said hello to them – even though it was impossible to talk, he made friends with them. The day got hotter, but not to the level it had been in the previous weeks, but certainly hot enough. The plains beyond Burgos are marked by motorways and roads and you're always aware that you are quite near, even after four or five hours, to this large city. It was a former capitol, under Franco, during the civil war and it's easy to see why. I'd bought a couple of t-shirts, and there was an ulterior motive. After being shunned by Beady Marie, and feeling generally wretched and lonely, I had made contact with Mariel. She was almost a client of my business from Oviedo in the north of Spain and I thought, what the hell, I'll make contact as she's literally the only person I know in the region. Amazingly we shared a short text conversation and she seemed keen to meet up. She really was lovely looking according to her online biog. I thought a couple of new t-shirts might be a good investment if we were to meet up. This is a good one, trust me, stick with it.

The Meseta is often spoken about as the place where pilgrims are forced to face their demons, a bit like Christ in the wilderness, except with hostels. It can take as much as ten or eleven days if you keep it to around twenty km per day. But here is where the mind takes over. You start realising that if it's twenty, and that it's pretty flat, then you can probably do twenty-five or twenty-eight and get it over with more quickly. Sometimes pilgrims would say, 'I loved the Meseta' and I wondered if there was something wrong with them. There's certainly little drama here, except what Huw and I created in our brains. I knew nothing about it until I was on the Camino. Even in the early days it was never a thing. When Huw started talking about it I thought it wouldn't be as flat and dull as all that. Most of it really was. After two or three days I had really spent a great deal of time confronting my demons and they're right, it's amazing what creativity one's brain can come up with when left to its own devices. When we got to Hornillos there were a good group of us in a hostel and we sat in a makeshift pool they had, sipping cans of beer and soothing our hot and sore feet. This was the first time I became more friendly with Tricia, a petit and warm American, Bonnie, a brassy Australian, and also AJ who I had met in Pamplona, and her partner Ady who I had met in Los Arcos, days before. Matthias was also there I think, and also possibly for the first time, Nico, although I can't swear to that, we'll find out more about him later. I went up to a bar further into the town and had a tortilla and beer then went back via another bar where Tricia and the others were. Older Matt was there too I think, from the night on the terrace. Then a short nap and down for the menu del dia, which was a very tasty paella. It always made the day if the hostel made an effort with the food, and in this case we all had huge portions whilst we sat at a long table. Huw was at one end with the Koreans and I was at the other end with the Aussies and the Americans. I must have had a few wines, which on top of the beer made me a bit lairy and in the end I gave an unprompted speech. I was feeling emotional and alone and I felt a drunken affinity with these people so I just made the point that we were from all over the world and it was fantastic and whilst most of the table had no idea what I was saying, I knew they'd understand Bon Camino – which they did. Then a bunch of us went on a pub crawl trying to find an open bar. There wasn't one, or rather there was if we had walked on another 500 metres where there was apparently a restaurant with cabaret... we eventually crashed and prepared for the early start the next morning, which I seem to remember, was the first with real rain facing us.

It ended after a short time, and there was a little excitement because it was cooler. I left my stick behind and went back for it. By this time, I think I was on my third, as others had taken my stick from the selection each morning so I had been left with theirs, but after so long, I couldn't be without one. Today's walk was a rural, green, not too stubbly walk to Castrojeriz. My memory of that walk is limited. About 5 km outside of the destination you arrive at an immense ruined abbey which has a small café and everyone stops for pictures under the ancient façade. The refreshment was welcome, and then on across more flatlands, in a sort of overcast day, in what felt a bit like Oxfordshire, towards an elongated village set into a vast cliff. If I had been feeling adventurous I would have walked up the cliff to see the view on top, but I wasn't. My hostel was at the furthest from the entrance to the village, it seemed to go on and on until I got there. Huw and Matthias were also at the hostel but I didn't see them until later. I remember feeling very hungry indeed and went across to a restaurant where I had steak and chips and some beer for not much money at all, then back to the hostel where I was in a room for eight and yet I was, and remained, the only person, which was a huge blessing. That evening's menu del dia was average, chicken and rice I think, and I know it wasn't enough for Huw. That evening was odd. I knew people around me, but I was tired, and didn't really want to seek out company. I slept pretty well due to the silence, and it rained again. Before dawn the next day I was up and walking as the sun rose, down towards a huge 600 metre incline that everyone was dreading. It was steep, but every hundred metres or so there was a place to stop to take in the view which grew behind you until the valley before you was so vast it took minutes to move your eyes from one side to the other. By the time I got to the top the clouds cleared for a little while and it was windy and beautiful. No iPhone photo can do justice to that view. It's a strong memory. It was just me. A few people walking by. Huw walked by in a big black waterproof like a huge black owl fighting his way along the path. He was cursing the mud that now clung to our boots. The plateau went on for many kilometres and would be the last hill we would climb for many a day. The rain came and went that day. I didn't mind it. I was wearing my jeans and my waterproof jacket that turned out to be a great investment, and with my hood over my baseball cap it kept the rain off my face, and I was snug in my soft jumper underneath. Eventually the plateau fell steeply away and I think this is where the flatness of the Meseta proper billowed out beneath. There were birds of prey above us, hanging there in the wind, looking for any signs of life. We were all heading for the town of Fromista. The lead in was quite long, along a canal and past a small monastery where you could stay but it was literally in the middle of nowhere. They'd feed you and wash your feet, which I know AJ and Ady did, the rest of us kept going. There was a boat which you could take for a couple of euros into the town. It's funny, at this point I didn't fancy it, but it would have been pleasant. Soon the canal twisted over a lock and you walked down into the town where a welcome café served yet another tortilla and a beer. I checked into the hostel and Huw and I went across the road to a café for a proper lunch which was very good, served by an amusing waiter.

Huw was suffering. He often came across as quite cantankerous, but he was in pain with this feet, and of course, he was doing this walk for very serious reasons which meant he was on a mission. It rained more – much more. We didn't need dinner after that lunch but anyway, I sat outside under the portico. Here Calamity joined me and we talked. I decided to just chat to her about what are the reasons why we do this walk, and it was lovely, emotional. She was a tiny woman but a powerhouse when it came to walking. There was a huge storm above us that turned the road into a river in seconds. The thunder was deafening. I think we had some cigarettes. I was smoking again, because of a difficult exchange I had had with K in Burgos which had stressed me, and this always made me want to smoke. Not when I was walking, but when I sat it gave me something to do and I loved the relief that the smoke gave me as it passed through my mouth and nose.

A little later I dodged the rain and went into the little pizzeria and joined Bonnie, AJ, Ady, Nico and Matthias at a table. We drank beer and ate snacks and I got a little tipsy. Bonnie, bless her, asked if I could give her a job if she came to the UK. I said something glib and patronising like 'send me your CV sweetheart...' and Matthias and Nico thought this was hilarious. We shared poems. I read some of mine, the early Sonnets in this book, and I became emotional because they were raw, written in the previous few days. I couldn't read the most personal ones, although I did read 'Tilting at Women' which they got I think. It was a lovely evening. I was so lucky to be included in their group. I now realise I was probably too old, but they never made me feel that.

**Fromista – Me, Ady, AJ, Bonnie, (all from Oz) Matthias (Belgium) and Nico (Germany)**

Many years ago, my friend Mark Siggers, a writer, contended that all poems must rhyme in some form. He obviously couldn't stand blank verse, and at the time I was much affected by this argument. So I decided in my late teens that, apart from a very few exceptions, my poetry output would largely take the form of Sonnets. Fourteen lines, 3 parts alternately rhyming (although they don't always and you can always use assonance) and then a rhyming couplet at the end. When I was at drama school I worked in a working-class club, and on quiet nights I would stand behind the bar using the receipt pad to write sonnets. Incredibly pretentious clearly, I mean to say, who the hell did I think I was? But that was the habit I got into – hence the Sonnets in this book.

    The warmth of that evening transferred to the hostel, where smiley Shelby from Japan/Taiwan was smiling at me as I got in, but then I hardly slept because of humidity and the rain outside storming away. I sat in a small room listening to the rain for a while, realising I wouldn't sleep again that night. From 5am everyone started getting ready to leave. Huw, who had as bad a night as me, joined me in the doorway and we both looked at the rain sheeting down. We looked at each other, and at the weather forecasts on our phones. I think we both said 'fuck this'. We went along to a café and had some breakfast and coffee, and I ordered a cab. At 9.30 a nice lady turned up and whisked us through the rain for a whole section. The route was straight along the roadside. We passed all of our friends who were gamefully walking in the torrents. They were all drenched. We had some feelings of guilt, but we had a cunning plan. We still planned to walk a stage but later, when it was dryer, and we knew that the stage we were missing was less than inspiring and even less so in the rain. At Carrion we had another coffee, saw some friends such as Elegant Cathy from Australia, and then we cracked on. Huw and I left the town – it was damp and not raining, and then we came to a long 17 km stretch that would take us to Ledigos. We split at this point because Huw needed some ditch focused privacy and I walked on. It rained again, not as heavily as in the morning, and this route was straight, flat, and bloody dull. We were walking at our own pace and knew we would meet later in the hostel. When it rained I had no choice but to wear my jeans which were loose fitting but still got heavy when wet. I had nothing else to wear except extra t shirts if it got very cold, so I just banked on that never happening. That straight line was very straight and quite long. It was interesting to me that Hugh wanted to walk separately but I didn't mind, it sort of worked for me. We didn't say anything he just went ahead in that very strident way of his whilst I strolled along as usual. It allowed me to listen to my playlist which was amazing at passing the time, and I looked at the grey clouds on top of us, watching the light in the distance as it slowly crept towards the east. This was Northern Spain after all, some of it looked quite English in its green lushness, or like bits of Ireland or Scotland. Of course, once, many millions of years before, it was all connected, so we shouldn't be so surprised when an area of Europe looks much like another area of Europe. The difference is often in architecture, like the very Spanish way they build some of their churches, just a hall, with a bell tower above, and unless it's something special, not a lot else. The herons and other birds build nests on the shoulders and the tops of the church bell towers, probably because they're so sturdy.

We're in the heart of Castile et Leon here, where colossal and bloody battles were fought between the Moors and the Christians. Where, once that fight was over they simply combined the region which it seems some aren't at all happy with. All along the way the signs for the region have one or the other name crossed through by the supporters of the other bit. So there's a separatist movement for Castile as well as Leon, and the Basque country through Gascony and Navarra and down towards Rioja, and of course Catalonia who voted for independence a few years ago. There was also some Welsh vandal who was writing on every sign he could find (I assume it's a he) the following; 'Cymru am Bith' which means Wales Forever, and is also the motto of the Welsh Guards, formed in 1915. So, a former Welsh Guard, or Welsh nationalist took it upon himself to have a challenge to write it all the way along, and it really annoyed the Welshman I was walking with. Huw is a pretty political person in Wales where he rails against the devolved assembly, the Tories, and anything else he feels strongly about online, but even he was 'fucking wound up' by the wanton and excessive act of continual vandalism. Sometimes it would ease and you thought that was it, then the next day there it would be on a sign showing you the way to Santiago. Anyway, the 17km stretch eventually got dryer, and we made it down a hill and around a sunny corner into Ledigos which is a minute place. There were two hostels, one of which is modern and nice, and one of which is family run and pretty grim, where we ended up. They offered private rooms for 20 euros which we had both booked and when we arrived we realised why. The guy running the place wore a thick black and white cardigan, this was late August, and he sold us a 12 euro menu del Pellegrino cooked by his mother, which we went for. I showered in a bath with rubber attachments on the taps – you remember? From the 1970s. And I had a private room with 2 beds. At least it was quiet. I went for a wander to the nice hostel and saw some pilgrims I recognised and had a beer there. Then back for a beer with Huw and dinner. It was unremarkable I seem to remember, with the rice pudding that is traditional for dessert. We concocted a brilliant film idea, where the guy here eventually got sick of his life and murders a pilgrim, and how the whole community agrees to say nothing about it. Then a clever detective turns up pretending to walk the Camino – genius. It would also work as a play. Set in the bar of this cheapo hostel. Huw and I did this a few times, creating plays and dramas from the different characters we were meeting. The Camino is one long drama of one kind or another. I digress, at the table next to us was a charming blonde German lady. We exchanged eye glances and that was clearly more than enough to guarantee that wherever she went after that on the Camino we were never destined to meet again. We drank some wine and went to bed early.

Did I say the room was quiet? As I got into bed I started to get comfy and then above me it began. The rat version of the Olympics. Whatever they were doing they were big, and loud, and I expected the thin plaster ceiling to cave in at any moment. It was a nightmare. Thankfully the exhaustion of technically completing 2 sections in one day (walking one) was enough to send me off to a fitful but undisturbed sleep.

Up at the crack I got ready and went down to the café. Huw had been and gone and that was fine so off I went after a coffee and a Napolitana (pain au chocolate). Huw told me later that in the half hour he was there, having a hasty espresso, a man walked in dressed in very scruffy clothes, had two large glasses of strong spirit which he sunk in seconds, and slouched off back to work. Maybe that was the only way to get through the day in that god forsaken place.

This was a sunnier day and I was back in my shorts, and today we were heading for Sahagun which is technically half way along the Camino Frances. This, in itself is an achievement. You can get a certificate (you pay for it) if you want one, to prove you've done it, but I thought, if you're going the whole way, what the hell? The walk takes you along some fields as usual, then some roadside walking – always pretty dull, until you eventually found your way to the diversion that takes you past a hermitage and then a monument to half way which is two statues. The one on the left is a pilgrim and the one on the right is a knight. Everyone gets their picture taken with the Knight. Then It's another 3-4km into Sahagun which is a fair-sized town. This takes you through the outskirts along the trainline and into the town which has a number of hostels. Huw and I walked the last seven miles or so together. We then checked into this hostel which was a collection of pallets winched halfway up a disused monastery wall, and they'd stuck a load of mattresses on the pallet bunks. The bottom ones you couldn't sit on, not enough headroom, and the top ones were okay just really high off the floor so if you fell off in the night you were in real trouble. We'd heard about some poor pilgrim on the Norte section who had done just that and been hospitalised. Still, we showered and agreed to meet later. I went for a drink, had a difficult chat with K who had got back in touch (hence the Sonnet at the start of the next chapter which was too personal, and I have had to replace it with a spare one, apologies) an exchange which I took reasonably well considering, and then I had a doze on the sky-high mattress before meeting the Welshman. Here was a man who was having problems.

So, we were talking quite rationally and then suddenly he shouted, 'fuck it!' or 'For fuck's sake!' – something like that and waved his arms in an exaggeratedly actor-ish fashion. I said 'What's the matter?' he suddenly stopped and looked at me. 'You don't know, do you?' 'Know what?' and he explained that he'd paid to see a doctor about his feet and his little toe was swollen and infected and the doctor had advised him not to walk on it at all for 3 days. It was so bad apparently that if he did carry on he would be unlikely to finish the walk at all. So, over some more beer and a long wait for dinner we chatted about his options. There was a train in the morning which would take him to Leon, and he could stay there in a hotel with a private room for a few days and rest up his foot. This was clearly the best option. I knew Huw was uncomfortable in the foot region but I had no idea he was in so much pain, poor guy. He was also suffering because of some unkind criticism from home, about what he was doing, why he was doing it and how he was going about it. As far as I could see Huw was doing something personal, discreet and effective, trying to create something positive from a very negative situation. But actors know, you can't please everyone. This brought him pretty low. I told him about my conversation with K and he advised me to stay well clear, which was good advice. Huw and I, I'll say this for us, were always direct with each other, as we will see more of in due course. I went online to see how his appeal was going and sure enough he was a few pounds off of £10k – incredible – so I was very happy to add the extra to take him over – he was pleased when it flashed up on his phone, and said so. After dinner we went to crash out on our raised mattresses, and I must say I was concerned Huw would roll out and damage himself still further. I sort of, hunkered up to the wooden bulkhead in the hope I wouldn't roll backwards – it was a stilted night, plus the 15 or so who were sleeping there all snored like drains which was amplified in the old church ceiling above us – pure hell. That morning he was gone early and we'd arranged to meet in 3 days' time in Leon. I had other ideas about this.

**Halfway – Sahagun.**

## Chapter 6. Sahagun to Leon

Bob's Camino Playlist Song: One for my Baby (and one more for the road) by Frank Sinatra

*'We're drinking my friend,*
*To the end, of a brief episode,*
*Make it one for my baby, and one more for the road'*

## Sonnet 6: Spare Sonnet

The stream runs on, nervous, among the blue
As my laugh, in the green shade, as your smile
As your squelching chatter above the boots,
As the hope settling for this gentle trial,
The stream runs on, so many odd questions,
Past, present, open, intimate, searching,
Flecks of white in the easy connection,
Nature, seducing, enveloping,
The stream runs on into fear, and my heart
Kicks the bells to shower me with limits
Testing my naïve soul before the start
Your warning, implicit in the tea leaves,
My life runs on, reflecting now your face,
Your life, changed I hope, by my warm embrace.


On the Buen Camino App, from Sahagun to Leon it said it

was 3 days hard walking across yet more of the flat,

recently harvested Meseta. I looked at the details and

realised that if I got my head down I could probably reduce

it to two days. The road was flat anyway, following motorways largely and I didn't like the thought of Huw languishing in Leon on his own for too long – and then hell of all hells – getting ahead of me. Strange that when you begin you don't give a shit when you finish or who you finish with, but then over time you form some kind of loose team, and maybe that's the human condition, we are meant, perhaps, to experience things together. Plus, the Meseta was dull enough by now, and on my own this was going to be totally depressing. So, on I went and by late morning had made it to the next night's stopover. The days walks were becoming easier, quicker. You didn't need to leave so early as it was cooler, and the land was flat so it was just trotting along, listening to the growing play list. So, this resolved me to keep going the next 12km, via a handy Tesla cab to Relegios. Another one-horse village with 2 hostels. Again, I chose the crapper one of the two.

This meant I was one days walk from Leon, and I was determined to be there the next night and had booked a lovely hotel room to celebrate. That afternoon in Relegios I went into the courtyard of the hostel for a beer and a fag and there were a British Couple I had observed from afar a couple of times. We said hello. They were fast these two, and were doing longer schleps than the rest of us. I was wary because I have never met the chap before, but Huw had warned me about 'another Englishman' who was on the walk, and I assumed this must have been him. They weren't staying in Relegios they were keeping going to the next town. I admired their commitment and said so. That was the first time we had spoken apart from waved greetings on the walk. They weren't staying there though, they were going further, and they looked like hardcore walkers who don't let anything like 'recommended daily distance' restrict what they're capable of. Strange that in the first 2 weeks I had thought the daily distances, if anything, were a bit too long, and now I also ignored them and thought about how far I could get, because I suppose, I was getting fitter.

I went for a wander around the village and had I gone into the other hostel I would have seen Bonnie, Kylie and some of the others for a drunken night in a bar, but I didn't. I ate a pretty nice 3 course meal and was in bed, on my own, and there was one Korean lady also staying there and we never crossed each other's paths. I lay in bed and watched crap on my phone, had a brief conversation with home as I remember, and then slept, only to be up early. We were left entirely alone in the hostel, which is a strange feeling. A couple of times I got up in the night for a wee, and it was entirely silent. Like being in an abandoned house.

The next morning I was up, along the motorway again and eventually walking through the town of Mansilla de Las Mulas. I would have stopped somewhere there but it was still early, not a lot was open, so I just kept going as I knew Leon wasn't that far. There was a little village further on which advertised a café open called Villamoros. I detoured into it only to find the café closed. Further up the main road I found a bakery where I was served by the most miserable sour faced woman on earth. I kept going and eventually near a dense wood was a donation café with souvenirs for sale where I had a banana and a cold drink. This was run by a pretty, happy lady, who sat at her lap top working, whilst keeping her eye on this little tarpaulined kiosk, which happily had a clean loo, with proper toilet seats etc. I was keen to get to Leon. I had booked a 4-star hotel and I wanted to sleep well and relax, and frankly, have a day off. So, I walked up through the next village and thought as I was near the city I might get a bus in. No luck sadly, there was nothing doing so I just kept going across more motorways and through an industrial estate. This was the worst of it really, not even a view, just concrete. I suppose it was inevitable that over a thousand years, some of the Way would become entirely deadly dull and built over, but it made you feel a little cheated that you had to endure it. Eventually you follow through a pass in the hills alongside the motorway and go past the hospital on the outskirts of Leon and there were regular buses. It was another 6km through concrete to get to the centre and I was happy for the bus to take me. A sweet Spanish lady helped me get the right bus and told me where to get off, which was lovely. Leon is very different to Burgos. Again, a proper modern city with a 'centro storico' (a historic centre) where I was dropped. As I entered I saw a bar where I immediately went in, and there I experienced 'bulls meat and bread' as a tapas with a beer. There were a bunch of Spanish gangsters in the bar who were having a few as well, there was a nice atmosphere. Soon I was in a lovely but small hotel room. The place had a bar on the roof with a spectacular view of the cathedral, which was one of the reasons I'd chosen it. After a good shower, and some time washing my meagre clothes, which I hung in the window to dry, I went for a wander. Leon was a lovely town. Everything centres around the cathedral and the roads around it where there are a myriad of shops, cafes and bars. I was on the rooftop bar having a beer and who should join me? Huw! He was much recovered and we were both due to continue in two days' time. Again, unspoken, we would go along, kind of as a pair, but if it became too much then he would slow down or stay somewhere after limited walking on his healing feet. He was impressed with my ability to get there when I had, and frankly so was I. We arranged for an early evening meeting with a group of pilgrims on the rooftop and it was here, later, that I met Jim and Beth, who were to become key figures, some of the Aussies Christine and Debs, two awful Englishmen whose names I have forgotten and who happily were finishing then in Leon, and Irish Kate who was a lovely lady who, although she was Irish, lived in Austria and as such had one of the strangest mixed accents I've ever heard. Jim was a retired chap from the US and enjoying his Camino. He was very white headed and bearded and very jocular and funny. I assumed he and Beth were partners, but no, they were just friends, travelling together on this strange path together. The Aussie ladies were open, funny, enthusiastic, and just the nicest people. Elegant Cathy was there, one of the prettiest ladies on the Camino, whom Huw had dubbed 'elegant' because of her long cracking legs and her general air of loveliness, and I agreed with him. It was lovely there on the roof, the circular window of the cathedral just across the way, and also the feeling that we had got somewhere and everyone was taking a day off the next day, so there was a half-term, holiday feel. I was also slightly more relaxed because Mariel, who was due to drive down to Leon from Oviedo to meet me, had blown me out, so that was that. I would be forced to relax and shut up about thinking about women. That evening Huw and I had a wander about Leon and went to a couple of bars and had snacks. It was a lovely town. I spoke briefly to two Italian girls who were enjoying a beer outside a bar. They had just arrived in Leon to go to university here, as part of the Erasmus Scheme, which means that you can attend any university in the EU and get funding for it through your own country's funding system. My son Harry, had asked me a year or so before, about going to a Dutch University and I had to tell him that due to Brexit that avenue of educational pleasure was now closed off unless you were prepared to pay through the nose for it. These two Italians were very excited to be starting their courses in Leon where they would be in international classes, enjoy the hospitality of the region and perfect their, no doubt, excellent Spanish at the same time. How lucky.

We all ended up in Huws hostel where they served us a pretty good menu del dia – after some wrangling with the owner and we ate pretty well, I think. I strolled back nicely hammered and had a final beer on the busy rooftop, and then went to my room to sleep deeply. I don't know why I went for that final beer. On the drunken off-chance, which is what it would have been, that some equally louche lady of any nationality would have taken pity on me in the small hours. Of course, I had been walking all day from Relegios, and was exhausted, but the feeling of the night, the excitement of being somewhere beautiful surrounded by people meant that my damaged brain was trying to dis-functionally throw me into harms or romances way. It fooled me into thinking that a glamourous Senora would find this Englishman fascinating and take pity on me. If she was there that night, we missed each other, I'm afraid. My hopes weren't high frankly and were almost immediately dashed. Thank god for a private room, and a cool night where the bed was comfortable and I could, probably, snore away without disturbing anyone except myself.

The next day was a day off. This was heaven. I got up late, showered at my leisure, hadn't paid for breakfast at the hotel on purpose, and went out, in clean clothes into the sunny morning. I sat at a café overlooking the cathedral and ordered coffee and a napolitana and was passed by many pilgrims including Bonnie who stopped for a chat, she was hungover too. I had hoped to see Ajay, Ady and maybe Matthias but they were a day or so behind. I was aware that they were consciously having their own pilgrimage, and didn't seem to be caught up in the slight sense of urgency that I had. I admire that inner strength.

After that I went on a long circuitous route around the old town. It was approaching lunchtime anyway, but I went down alleys, found squares with little cafes, and larger piazzas with restaurants and the air of a day off was hanging all around it. It was a Friday and people were finishing work at lunchtime and getting ensconced in the bars. It was a very relaxing day. I eventually found another square where there was an excellent small tapas bar and I stood at the bar and had a couple of beers with yet more stewed beef (bulls' beef?) sausage, and a type of tapenade on bread which was lovely with beer. The counter had lots of shellfish, fish and other delights available, but I didn't fancy that – it was almost too far inland. Over the bar was a gentleman getting nicely tanked up on what looked like iced red wine. I watched him being topped up with more red, and then asked the barmaid if it was indeed chilled red. Of course it wasn't – it was iced red vermouth! So, I had one of those. This, on top of the beer and not too much to eat made me pretty pissed. I really missed the family at this point. In the past on holidays, we always ended up in bars or restaurants, it was what we enjoyed. I sent messages and got some response. I was missing them despite the booze, everything in my life seemed a long way off in every sense. I hoped they understood how much I loved and missed them.

  I staggered out a little later and dragged myself up to the cathedral where I was angling for a stamp on my Compostela. The cathedral was large, and had the most incredible stained glass windows of every colour. As I was drunk these seemed even more amazing than perhaps they might, and I took many pictures. There were also lots of old gargoyles and stone turrets in the courtyards and quads and this was impressive but ultimately, I was glad I wasn't suffering the guided tour that many were on. As I got my stamp at the other end of the cathedral, I knew I needed a nap so I repaired to my room for just such a luxurious moment.

**Day off in Leon – Bar crawl (previous page), Red Vermouth and a psychedelic Cathedral.**

Later, I emerged and went to meet the others at a hostel down the road, which was where they were having a birthday party for someone – there was Alisha and Richard, yet another couple who weren't a couple but were just travelling together, and an American lady whom I never saw again and a Korean lady who had a puppet teddy bear which was the only thing she would talk through... if you addressed her, she spoke back through the puppet in a silly high-pitched voice. Quite bizarre and for a while I put it down to the vermouth. Huw and I exchanged a few knowing glances at this point. Jim and Beth went off for mass at the cathedral (they were Catholics) and then Huw and I went on another crawl for an early dinner which we managed in a nice restaurant. I must say I was pretty tanked and exhausted at this stage. The streets were becoming far busier too. Here in September on a Friday evening all of the bars spilled out into the street and crowds of people were standing around drinking, smoking and chatting. Everyone was dressed smartly and all of the women were done up to the nines. I would have loved to be there with someone special. It had a great atmosphere, and there was a feeling of 'weekend' emanating from every corner. I really liked Leon, and the thought of departing the next day for a less luxurious hostel was painful for me. Having said that, it was lonely to be there without any love interest in my life whatsoever. There was literally no one I could share this experience with, no one I could legitimately connect with, even. Loneliness is odd and hard when it strikes you. I would have loved to have been with a pretty lover, holding hands as we darted between bars, chatting to groups of nice Spanish people, explaining that we were newly in love, looking at each other across the busy pathways in a silent language that only we could understand, but my hand stayed empty that evening and I had no idea when anyone's would be holding mine again. It's being hard on yourself. The Camino tries it's best across the Meseta to help you better deal with being alone, but in the end, it is work you need to do on your own, when others are around, all looking at you with a certain level of vagueness because you're the stranger who is there alone and they are the locals taking this social life for granted as I walk back to my accommodation alone. On the roof terrace there were some beautiful people enjoying their evening, some very beautiful. In my sink washed t shirt and only pair of loose jeans I must have looked very scruffy to them.

That night I packed my bag as much as I could and laid out my walking gear for the morning. I knew I had lost weight in the intervening weeks. I also knew I was in the final two weeks of the walk and this startled me – this was going very quickly indeed. I had a few more days officially, of the Meseta, and then up from Astorga, into the mountains again and finally, Galicia and Santiago. Castile and Leon was a massive area to have crossed, and most of it, other than the cities, I would not miss.

I have been criticised by other pilgrims for venturing this opinion. For that is what it is. If you like the flat dull crap of the Meseta then jolly good luck to you, but please don't look at me (or have a go at me on social media) as though there is something wrong with me for finding it so boring. There are some who will not have a word said against any particular element of the Camino, (especially on social media) as if it is a sacred route that cannot be criticised because it is so perfect. It's a truly wonderful, life changing experience, but for anyone, there will be elements which are pretty damned far from perfect. And as I've said – this is my opinion. Some think I'd mention this to put people off, far from it. This manuscript, so far, is 100% the truth and will remain so and if people disagree then let them write a book to contradict me, and I'll accept it's their opinion too. Later, at Sarria, we will see what comes from overstepping general criticism into downright heresy!

Everyone, including Jim and Beth, and the Aussies were all keen to get out of the city environs as quickly as possible the next day, and not spend 2 hours walking out through the modern town. We had all discussed it and apparently the route out of Leon was almost as built up and depressing as the way in and there was a single bus at 8am that would get us about 8km along, and outside of the city, dropping us in a village called Las Virgen del Camino, to then take up the walk again. This suited Huw with his healing toe, and I also then resolved to walk on further than him that day because I could, to another village and that place was called Hospital d'Orbigo.

Jim, don't know, Chris, Elegant Cathy, Alisha, Richard, Boring bloke, Debs, Sandra, Lovely Beth and Huw. Leon Cathedral behind.

**Chapter 7. Leon to Foncebadon**

Bob's Camino Playlist Song: Am I Wrong by Anderson Paak

'I'm only out to play
Nothing more that I hate in this life
The wrong impression
I only have one to make
You can open your palm
Waiting to catch a break
The cards will fall where they may
And what about me?
I believe in fate
They wanna know where I'll be in five?
What about today? What about tonight?'

**Sonnet 7: What people are carrying (for Alec)**

Every face is a façade, a mask,
Overcompensating, hiding the truth,
Do we ask? Do we wait? Will they tell us?
Will faces change, with each step of the foot?
Habit forces a rush to quick judgement
So, we avoid, walk on, steer clear and hide
Because our own burdens are more private,
Less valid, unworthy or too painful?
Time and chance brings us sudden pain and guilt
As we see inside the pilgrims warm soul
And we compare them to our own poor heart
And wish them well for their personal goal
For every weighty pack on our sore backs
Each heart is as heavy with life's sadness.

This is where the Camino changed for me significantly in many ways. It's going to get emotional, dear reader, and I make no apology for that. I knew this journey would give me a shake up and change me. By god, though, I did not know, that damp morning in Leon, what was coming.

The bus out for 8km was genius. We missed the worst of the rain and the sun tried to poke its head out. It was good to be walking again although largely, once again, at the roadside. I walked with Jim and Beth for a bit until they slowed, and Huw was desperate to be off and stormed away like an immense beetle in his black waterproof poncho.

There was an alternative route – I met a pretty lady who was taking it and it was now I was beginning to realise that there are many, perhaps slightly more scenic options off of the main drag of the Camino, but you need to know about them in advance so you can plan it in. It was a pretty easy 10km via a café (quite a souvenir focused café with higher prices...) to get to Saint Martin. This is where Jim, Beth and Huw were staying. Huw had to take it easy on that first day back after his enforced rest and was happy to stay in the quite lovely Hostel we had arrived at for coffee etc. Jim and Beth had private rooms booked all the way along, they had booked them in advance, so they always knew where they were staying but this didn't give them much flexibility. I bade them farewell and continued alone on to Hospital d'Orbigo. This was another 10km and I'm sorry to say it was pretty much all roadside, and occasionally it rained so much that I had to change into different clothing and put the bag cover over my pack. On the walk I was passed by all my new and younger friends, Bonnie and the girls from the US, the Italians and older Matt whom I was coming to know well.

When we arrived at Hospital it wasn't exactly hospitable. We had all chosen a hostel on the other side of town and this meant crossing a huge bridge with many arches across the Orbigo river. It was sheeting down now, however I could see a restaurant on the other side of the river so I set my sights on that and stomped across in the rain. It's a really long bridge, endless arches and the rain was following me all the way. As I entered the sanctuary of the restaurant, like a drowned rat, I was brusquely informed by the owner in his waistcoat that they were closed... Not the expected welcome for a genuine pilgrim currently supporting the local economy. So, I was forced to carry on to the hostel, another twenty minutes walk. Casa Verde was named so for a reason. We checked in, in a very cool, hippy style room where everyone was waiting to get into their rooms and showers after the horrendous wet walk. Eventually, soon, I was shown downstairs to a room with 6 others, and a shower, which I took. Older Matt was in a private room.

I should explain that I was carrying in my pack a quick dry towel which folded up very small, which cost the earth to buy, but meant you could dry yourself very quickly, and then the towel would dry very quickly, and something like this is worth the money when you have a small rucksack (twenty-six litres) like mine.

There was a roadside bar we were told, over by a roundabout, so I walked up there for a few beers and Matt joined me. He was a pleasant chap from Vermont, a widower. We had a couple of beers, and maybe he had a wine – the weather made it that kind of a drinking day. This was the second time Matt had walked the Camino Frances. He knew all of the routes, the short and long cuts and the routes with better views, but he didn't ram it down your throat. He always slept in private rooms because of his snoring, and I envied him his foresight because he must, always, have slept well. I had some cigarettes which I smoked in the garden of the Casa.

I should explain that I would regularly try ringing home to speak to my sons which generally meant me asking questions and them uttering short answers. I missed them. At one point, I wanted my older son to fly out and meet me, but he couldn't see the purpose, and in hindsight, I think it would have been beyond him. However, I think for him and all young people this walk would alter their perspective on life hugely.

The girls all did a Yoga class, good for them. I think I napped for a bit before we went for dinner. The entire population of the hostel sat in this room around several tables. The staff sang us a song of thanks or of welcome, I'm not sure. At first it was charming but within a minute it had gone on too long, and we were starving. The song went on forever, and sounded like the kind of song you were taught at a second-rate kindergarten as a punishment. Of course, Casa Verde means... it was a vegetarian meal, which was fine. Rice always fills you up and it was certainly tasty enough using locally grown vegetables but only drinking water as I recall – no wine. Luckily, I'd eaten some meat snacks with Matt at the garage café. I chatted to the Americans on my table and we got to know each other some more. Tricia, it so happened, was single. As was Nicole – as was Bonnie. These ladies are all twenty years at least younger than me and there I am calling Matt older.

    Tricia was very easy to speak to. I told her about my tragic love life, and she listened sympathetically which is what real friends do. I apologised to her for the tale of woe and she said, 'hey don't worry Bobby – I love talking to you.' Thanks Tricia that meant a great deal.

These young people were very inspiring – on career breaks and having some direction in their lives where here I was searching for mine. I liked them all, they were good people, as well as being self-motivated in a way that I never was at that age. The nicest thing about the meal was that it was donativo, which means make a donation in the morning when you leave, which we did, but it was a lower cost meal as a result. No wine though...

I had a dreadful night's sleep in the Casa, due to a full room of snorers. In that room was also Christian whom I met later and his lovely blonde female travelling companion (they were both Swiss) whom I remembered, had walked 40km from Burgos in one day the week before. At dawn the next day most people were up and about and I left through the corn field behind the Casa. The breakfast was some home-made vegan bread which was dry, dark brown and unpalatable and some homemade jam which was questionable. Luckily, I was able to get a cup of instant black coffee (no dairy in the place) which gave me some kind of lift. We'd been warned to close the gate because of the dogs who would have followed us all the way to Astorga, which was the next big town. Straight ahead and right, then all the way up to the scenic path which led away from the Hospital. I was also not too miffed about the terrible night's sleep I had experienced because I knew I had a hotel waiting in Astorga, a hotel that had…. a Spa!! Oh, you devil Bobby!

I loved this day's walk, it was very memorable for me. I suppose over 2 weeks into the walk, you know a few people, and you're more practiced at what you are doing and it becomes more enjoyable overall. Firstly, I walked with Deb and Chris, the two Australian ladies and maybe Elegant Cathy, but I can't be sure. Then later it was Tricia – we walked together for a while and I gave her some more of my tragic love life stories (poor thing) which I think she found highly amusing. She then went ahead, (unsurprisingly) as these younger ones are apt to. The good news was that the landscape was challenging, some steepish hills, and it was beautiful views all around. I also knew that Huw was bringing up the rear after a night in St Martin and was planning on being in Astorga that evening. The landscape was scrubby, mossy and gorsy, but with sweeping hills in the distance. The land rose without too much of a climb up to a tree lined plateau that levelled out for a while and we all met up again at a donativo refreshment stop outside a remote house which offered drink and fruit and food. The food was all help yourself as the dad of the commune, a cool hippie in sandals and loose clothing, sat there strumming his guitar and playing with his kids whilst pilgrims tucked into his offerings and put a few coins into his box in the middle of the serving table. I think it's nice when people set these places up, like the lady in the woods near Belorado, but the table was covered with flies and wasps which rendered the food pretty unappetising. I wasn't that bothered as I knew I'd be in the town by the early afternoon, so I grabbed a banana which couldn't be contaminated, and made my way onwards. The road narrowed through woods which were unremarkable, and quiet, until at last you could see Astorga in the distance. It really didn't look that far and a bronze pilgrim on the hillside taking a drink, showed me so. You walked down into the suburbs, across a river, and then on towards the trainline. The way took you to a bridge which had clearly been built in error. It was cast iron and went over two tracks of railway running parallel. The bridge was a continuous zig zag which looked like a mistake that they'd only spotted halfway through building it. It was immensely long and you spent ages going up one side, effectively three times to get to the top, then over, then the same 3 pointless routes down to the other side. It was then uphill into the old town.

**Astorga**

Astorga was the joining of several Caminos, from the North and the South, as well as ours. Walkers would be arriving from Seville – further than the Route Frances that I was walking, and from the North, down from Oviedo, or from walking the Norte which went along the coast, so I imagined that it would become a little busier. It was an uphill schlep into the town which was quite highly placed. It had been the place of another siege during the Napoleonic wars and again, you could see why because of its high position. As I scaled the hill towards the hotel I was stunned to see many, many souvenir shops. Now, loads of little kiosks sold souvenirs here and there and it had increased since Leon, but this was almost industrial. The sort of shops you see on the sea fronts of Spanish seaside resorts now populated the main street in this town and sold Camino fridge magnets and t-shirts. I found this went against the principle of what we were doing. I don't resent the requirement but there was one next to another. Once again, my heresy runs the risk of being shouted down by Camino purists. This is a theme we will return to.

At my hotel I had time to wait before my room was ready. This was how early it was – it was lunchtime after all. So, I left my bag and went up to a bar opposite the lovely cathedral, and a building designed by Gaudi the Spanish architect which I should have been more interested to go into, but wasn't. I am sorry to say I had had quite enough of cathedrals, and I didn't go into that either. The bar opposite did a truly excellent tortilla and beer and I had some of this to assuage my hunger. I came out feeling nicely tipsy and anxious to use the spa. My room was comfortable and quiet and I changed into my hitherto unused swimming trunks and the hotel robe, and made my way to the spa which had a pool, sauna and jacuzzi. There was a mother and daughter using it, and it always feels slightly odd when it's very quiet – but it was lovely. I had a great sauna, very hot, then swam and then lay in the jacuzzi letting the bubbles soften my rock-hard feet and massage my poor body. My god this felt amazing. I can't tell you how wonderful it was to be somewhere focused on relaxation after so much effort, and walking and moving, and looking at timings and distance, I was instead in a civilised hotel, not nearly as nice as Burgos but certainly by any hostels' standard, lovely. I think I had a nap on the bed afterwards – much needed after the rough night at Casa Verde, and I was looking forward to eating something that night – and it would be meat, I knew that. Later I walked down from the hotel to a larger piazza and met Huw. We embraced and sat in a bar drinking beer and snacks, and we were joined by different faces from the walk, including for the first time in a few days, Shelby and her spider like chap. In time Jim and lovely Beth joined us.

They were a really friendly couple in their clean and sparkling gear. Although remember, they weren't a couple. They were college friends who were walking together and had left their respective spouses at home. Huw and I were having a couple of dirty burgers as I remember, could have been something else. It was funny how after a couple of weeks everyone was getting used to seeing us, the Camino Double Act, who between us knew so many people along this strange road. I tell you this, it felt good to have a friend. Someone to share this with. His partner and daughter knew about me which was nice when he was speaking to them, and we could really talk about anything, His voice was so like Tony, my late friend whom I missed often, and he had a similar approach to life. His toe was greatly improved although he was measuring more carefully his daily walk. He'd walked much further than me that day from St Martin, whereas I had only come from the

Hospital, about 18km, so he'd done a good 28 and was clearly on the mend. Jim mentioned it was Beth's birthday the next day, so I made a mental note and bought her a little trinket in the souvenir shop – nothing much, a small bracelet with a silver shell, just a dum-dee-dum. After some more beers and saying hello to Alisha and Richard, we went to our respective hotels.

The only real lack was romance. I had no current prospects. I felt alone romantically and were it not for my Camino friends I should have felt very lonely indeed. I couldn't really see where my next love, if ever, would arrive. Having said that, there was something germinating. A few weeks before I had left I had been introduced to a beautiful Scandi artist. I'd followed her on Instagram but that was it. Her posts on social media were always very upbeat and positive, and colourful. At one point I sent her a message simply saying, 'thanks, your posts are really motivational.' This was a few days before when I was on my own in the Meseta which was a measure of the loneliness. I would even try contact with a complete stranger for company! She responded and complimented me on walking the Camino, so we had begun a little correspondence, nothing more, but at this point I was immersed in my walk and she was a stunner anyway, I felt sure she was clearly, again, out of my league. Are you noticing a pattern here?

I had another quiet night in a hotel, and after opting for no breakfast I thought I'd leave early for a walk up a new mountain that would take me over towards Ponferrada. It was a good 28km walk the next day, but it would put me nearer the summit of the mountain if I made the walk and after the comparative luxury of the hotel I was ready to stretch it a bit.

This walk had so many facets to it. The first route out of Astorga was cold and a bit damp and not too inspiring. In the distance the famous cathedral spires were visible for miles, breaking the red dawn beyond, quite beautiful. And as the roadside walking changed we started going through villages with cafes and stops, and lovely paths and rural communities amongst them, and it was certainly busier, no doubt. Bonnie stomped past me a couple of times walking alone, and she really was a compelling sight in her Wonder Woman walking bikini. There was a defiance in her face that was very inspirational, and also her smile was big and broad, with sparking eyes. I was so glad to have met this special person, who like some of the others didn't seem to mind me. Again, I was largely walking alone, I saw Jim and Beth at one point, and Huw, and Calamity, god knows where she had come from, and Chris and Debs and many others. Over time, the walk started to rise gently into foothills, heathland, and it was cloudy. Some of the villages started to be laid out over steep cobbled streets that pushed you upwards. Once more, as the height increased, the view behind you, leading back to Astorga, widened in its grey and red and blue colours, adding an intensity and I found myself turning more often to look at it. One lovely village was a straight path, with cafes all along and I stopped randomly at one where a Dutch chap served me coffee. He was an ex-pilgrim who had loved the Camino so much that he had bought this café and moved his family here, to live in the region and to spend his life serving and being surrounded by pilgrims. He was a very proactive man, planning a pilgrim's festival. Great idea. Imagine walking the Camino and timing it to coincide with a music festival full of pilgrims? Great thought. He had a carving of Don Quixote outside his café and it reminded me of Tony (my late actor friend) who had played Sancho Panza in a production of this story opposite the great Paul Scofield, in London. This friendly chap also showed me a diagram to illustrate the point that there were mountains after the Cruz de Ferro, where we were heading next, but nothing as high. So, I felt again, and this was confirmed by conversations with older Matt, that I was speeding up, and the last few weeks were going to go very quickly indeed. This was the first time I became aware of the Cruz de Ferro but had no idea what it was.

I walked onwards and upwards again after an intense coffee, still many kilometres to go. In time, we arrived at a village where almost everyone, now the sun was out, was stopping for lunch. I also stopped for something – tortilla probably and I chatted to Nico, who to my surprise, was carrying a brick. He had a burger. It was here at this place that we chatted, and he smoked a cigarette. This was a young man, who had walked a long way from Germany to be here. There was some sort of issue with his mother that he was getting away from. I asked him about the brick. This heavy, large, engineering style brick I'd noticed him carrying along the way. He was going to leave it, the next day at the Cruz de Ferro. I didn't know what this was. In fact, I was probably the only pilgrim who had no idea what he was talking about.

The Cruz de Ferro – the iron cross – is a small cross on a large pole. Nobody knows where it came from and there are various theories that contend it was placed there to mark the highest point. Around it are thousands of stones. Those stones are brought from all over the world by pilgrims who leave them there. Many represent people who have been lost to the pilgrims; mothers, partners etc, who had died, and the stone has been brought from a house or garden in another part of the world to be left there under the iron cross. Other versions state that if you take a stone and throw it over your shoulder you are metaphorically, casting your burdens onto the pile, and leaving them behind you. I liked the sound of this, and also couldn't understand why I knew nothing about it. At this point Alec and Dawn walked up, the afore mentioned Brit. I hadn't seen them I think since before Leon, and Alec came straight up to me.

'Hi there, you're Bobby, aren't you?

'Yes' I responded, and I looked at him, he looked quite red-faced and emotional. We talked briefly about what was coming up, I think I explained that I didn't know about the Cruz de Ferro, and he looked at me directly and pulled a small white stone from his pocket and showed it to me. It had the word 'Claire' written on it. Alec explained 'It's for my wife who died a couple of years ago, I'm walking this for her.'

I have to say this hit me like a brick. I was moved to tears, I didn't know what to say. I felt a human, fundamental sympathetic stiletto of grief enter my mind and body. I felt so ashamed. I felt so sad.

This is a lesson I still muse on. How can we judge anybody we don't know, what right do we have? It's a habit, it's self-defence but it also comes from a nature that sets us apart for the wrong reasons. The truth is that you never know what anyone is carrying inside, which is why we should always be kind. Why has this taken me 53 years to realise? This realisation has changed me and continues to. It inspired the Sonnet at the beginning of this chapter.

The Cruz de Ferro is at over 1500 metres, the highest part of the Camino, and then you descend over a thousand metres to get to Ponferrada. For many the Cruz is one of the highlights. For me, in my ignorance, I was the heretic who didn't believe the magical significance that they were all looking forward to. By god, I had some burdens. Would the Cruz de Ferro do the trick for me?

Huw, and Alec and the Aussie girls were staying there in that lower village whereas I had opted to go on another 6 or 7 km uphill to Foncebadon. This village is mentioned in Paulo Coelho's book *The Pilgrimage*, near where he has a fight with a rabid dog which represents all of the internal demons he was battling on his Camino. The dog's name is Legion. The battle is very vivid and of course, it is also a battle with himself, so do any of us win battles like that? I sensed that my own battles were just starting.

I was looking forward to seeing it – it is near the top of a mountain and snow covered in winter. The route up is pretty steep and very rocky, I lost my footing a couple of times plus it rained a bit so was even more slippery. Although it was the highest mountain, after three weeks of walking, compared to the Pyrenees I was hopping up this hill. I listened to my music and saw this steep route as a proper challenge. I knew the super-fast American girls had flown on ahead and I knew that Jim and Beth were heading up there too, so I would see others when I got there. Once more, as I scaled this hillside, the backdrop continued to widen until I could see for many miles back past Astorga, seeing distant land that I had already travelled across. This seemed miraculous. As I walked, I kept up a fairly constant heavy pounding on the road, as if I was punishing myself. Who would I leave a stone for? My family? People I had hurt? My late father? My other relatives and friends who had died? Tony, my best friend? There were so many people I could leave a stone for. Too many. I thought about Alec and his burden, this thing that had spurred him on over hundreds of miles. I thought of my burdens, invisible, but weighing down on me far more heavily than my pack. So many to name and most of my own making. I stooped and picked up a white piece of rock, and wiped it in the rain. This small stone would come to represent my burdens, such as they were, and also perhaps, the burdens I had inflicted on others. Perhaps this supernatural place would somehow relieve these individuals. I'm not religious. I don't believe that the Cruz de Ferro is a sacred place because if I did then I would be admitting that I accept that there are sacred things and I really don't. However, I liked the idea of people cleansing themselves by leaving something of themselves at this high place and turning their back on it and walking away from it. Then it ceases to have a hold on you, and perhaps it frees your mind, through that act of casting a stone. You surely don't need the religious aspect to make it real? Your own mind can do that for you. Paulo, in his books, talks about being brave enough to say goodbye to something and then life rewards you with new 'hello'. I believe this idea of making your own luck. People of faith will contend that everything is part of god's plan. I prefer coincidence, I always have.

The way was tougher as it got wetter and more slippery and my stick became more essential for stopping me slipping over. It was funny how, now that the weather had changed entirely and we were in more unpredictable regions, I had come to accept it and actually not mind a bit of rain at all. It gave you an energy boost to try and get out of it. The path meandered alongside a steep road going upward, and you hopped up crumbling pathways to get to the next level. I remember feeling emotional and motivated as I walked. I knew that Nico was carrying his huge brick and it represented his relationship with his mother, and it was a massive thing for him to leave behind. I thought of poor Alec who was walking this for Claire, and loyal Dawn, a true friend, who was sharing this experience with him. And of course, dear Huw, walking for his nephew, where he would be leaving something of that memory behind. Their causes were so much more real than mine. Mine was my own cause, my own journey caused by my own actions. My inability and cowardice many years ago to act, my depression and how I over compensated, my affair and subsequent heartbreak, and all the anguish and pain I had caused for so many people, especially those I loved and would never be able to reconcile with. My burdens were things I deserved – so how could I cast them off? Wasn't this walk all about that? To somehow find this act of rebellion, as a line in the sand of my life so I could start to move on? If I couldn't believe that I deserved the luxury of releasing my burdens, then maybe I could be there for others. Maybe that was my purpose. As a Samaritan there is a small amount of satisfaction you receive if a caller thanks you for listening. That's our privilege. I would make myself more available to listen. This was a significant change for me, and some of you will be thinking, 'wow you selfish bastard has it taken you that long?' Well yes, I'm sorry to say it has, but better late, than never.

Eventually the tough path moved ever upwards into this small hamlet really, – not much more, with several hostels and a couple of restaurants and a bar. A blonde attractive lady checked me into her hostel and I was in a loft room sharing with about eight others. She did some washing for me for a few euros and I showered. I think I had a brief chat with K. She wasn't in a very good place but I tried to be forgiving and tried to make her smile by explaining the beauty of my surroundings, the immense view down the mountain and the place I was about to go to in the morning. It's a hard thing to take it in, and I think you really need to do something like this, to appreciate it at all.

I had a nap and a beer. I had an online chat with my Scandi contact which was nice. There was the attractive Swiss lady, I've forgotten her name, who slept near me and she was travelling with Christian who I am sorry to say was a bit smelly. I thought they were together but again, no. Just walking friends, and after that night I never saw them together again.

The girls, Tricia, Nicole and Bonnie and Nico the chap from Germany, were around. Eventually we met for a menu del dia – unremarkable I think, and had a couple of drinks. We laughed a lot about something that evening, there was an atmosphere that tomorrow was some huge near fatal challenge we were all facing. After dinner I sat on the back stoop smoking and looking at the view. They all had stones they were carrying and nobody really said much about how they would approach the Cruz the next day. I had a feeling they would be there earlier than me. I went up to the larger hostel in the village and met Jim and Beth who were all at dinner with the lovely Aussie ladies. I gave Beth my little trinket and she put it on her wrist and was quite touched I think. She told me about her family, her daughters and we all sat there laughing together. After the emotional damage I had been through all day this was good. Poor Jim had lost his mother-in-law and a brother that year and he had pictures to leave at the Cruz de Ferro. We arranged to meet the next morning at 8 as it was only twenty minutes up to the cross and we wanted to be there in daylight. Beth was going to come with us then get a cab down to Ponferrada because the steep inclines were bad for her legs. I had a beer and then we said good night. Back at the hostel I had a late-night chat with K. She was the nearest thing I had to someone I could hug. Whatever was said, was brief.

In the end I fell onto the put-you-up that I was sleeping on and had a few hours sleep – no more. It was a disturbed night in that loft. At least I had clean clothes and I would get breakfast in the morning as I wasn't leaving till later than usual. Walking every day for 25km does tire you. I was up a mountain in a tiny place, a medieval village where knights and Moors had fought years ago. I was surrounded by snorers and couples and bike riders. I was alone but had friends nearby. I was desperate for love, I know I keep saying that. To be loved. To hug my wife, my boys, my friends. I was desperate to find something positive from what I had done to my life, but there just wasn't one and I had to accept that and try to imagine this as the start of something new.

That bed was one of the most uncomfortable, and what sleep I got was limited. I got up in the night and went downstairs for a while. I really felt alone. I was a long way from anywhere that was familiar. There was nothing above me, here, everything was behind or below, perched as I was on the side of the highest peak of the entire Camino. I knew Huw was 8km behind and his toe would preclude him from catching me up for a day or so. I couldn't attach myself to the younger girls, in the same way, and I wouldn't. There was something about the Cruz de Ferro, now I knew about it, that made me nervous. What if my burdens refused to be left there? My ignorance about this place clearly singled me out as somebody who lacks any spiritual capacity to plan for it. I should have bought a stone from my garden in Kent, a piece of hard Bethersden Marble and left that at the foot of the cross. As perhaps other English pilgrims had done before. Instead, I had a small white stone, a very insubstantial thing to represent all the things that it now did. For me it would be symbolic, for others they would invoke their God to take their burdens. The next day would be long, hard, emotional. It also turned out to be quite, quite magical and I will never forget it.

**Hard going – the Way to Foncebadon.**

**Chapter 8. Foncebadon to Villafranca**

Bob's Camino Playlist Song: Speak Low by Sammy Davis Junior

*'Our moment is swift,*
*Like ships adrift,*
*We're swept apart,*
*Too soon,*
*Speak low, darling, speak low,*
*Our love is a spark, lost in the dark,*
*Too soon, too soon.'*

**Sonnet 8: Jim and I**

Two friends shared a unique experience
Riding the clouds, from above in the sun,
Sharing our griefs, relieving our burdens
Pilgrims, sliding down an endless mountain.
Through to rocky descents and welcome beers
Sometimes chatting, sometimes waiting, watching,
Checking the distance from the Cruz de Ferro
Where we left behind our hearts hard beating
Supporting as good pilgrims always do,
Along the strange road to Santiago
Laughing as friends should, as Beth takes a cab,
Falling into a bar, (it was hot work)
The beers were so cold, ice floated on top
Memories made, two gents, ready to drop.


At breakfast opposite the Swiss non-couple, I

complemented her that she hadn't snored and she was

delighted. After a Napolitana (chocolate croissant) and a coffee I bade farewell to the nice hostel lady and stalked up to the larger hostel where Beth and Jim were ready. We were a little quiet. We had some idea about what was coming. The mountain went up through trees and followed the road. It was fresh and sunny – the most beautiful morning with blue sky and sun everywhere, if I think of that morning, at any time, I am moved. We were above the clouds here as we approached the iron cross. 1500 metres above sea level.

What you hope, of course, is that you will arrive there and experience the thing alone. On the Camino that's unlikely. As we approached there were Korean girls standing in front of the cross taking pictures. I found this very odd – for me it just wasn't that kind of place. The act of picture taking was too commercial for this place – this place demanded peace and quiet. As they eventually moved away, I thought, what the hell and threw my stone onto the pile, over my shoulder, and felt my burdens lift. Not really – maybe a little. The action felt relatively insignificant. I then stepped back to the fence to let Jim and Beth have their time. Beth didn't take too long and stepped away, but poor Jim was struggling. I had removed my pack and was standing there, when he leaned forward and rested his hands on his knees, shaking with emotion and I just reacted. I went over and put my arms around him and we hugged. He was very emotional of course. In this special place he was confronted by his losses and was grieving anew. I was honoured to be there for him. Thankfully I could help someone. Someone I didn't know that well, but it didn't matter. At that moment I would have hugged anyone at all.

After a little while we stood away and let others have their time. Soon after the cab arrived, and Beth was in two minds whether to leave us. She did though. Jim, I think, wanted to few hours in different company, which is fair enough, especially when you're not travelling with your wife, and that was fine with me. We never discussed it we just knew we'd walk together that day. And what a walk. I'm filling up now just thinking about it. As we started down the other side of the mountain, the sun was high and the views all around were breath-taking, every peak underlined by a pure white line of clouds. We walked at a similar pace. And without discussion we just accepted, sometimes he'd go ahead, then I would, it didn't matter, sometimes we'd walk together. A few kilometres on, still above the clouds, there was a van offering drinks and we stopped for coffee. Bonnie, Tricia and Nicole were there and some younger American girls who were just loving the views and the purity of this area. Jim and I sat in the sun, we were happy. In that day Jim became my friend.

Someone, a stranger, a pilgrim like me, whom I did not know before and now someone I will know for the rest of my life – like Huw. When I think about that moment enjoying the coffee, I was very happy, very lucky, so damned fortunate. Maybe the loss of my burdens were the best thing I could have done? In the end, as I have said – we are all carrying something. If I could recreate that walk again, I would not change a single thing about it. It was perfect for so many reasons.

After the café we descended along rocky pathways going through scrub bushes and through woodland until we reached the cloud line. Imagine that, walking for miles above the clouds. Surrounded by hillsides and peaks, and views that were unique and beautiful.

Then suddenly you were walking through the cloud. A faint moisture was clinging to my legs as the sun was obscured for a few minutes as we walked through. This gave way to a new village and a bar. It was mid-morning now and Jim bought us a beer. There was Shelby and other friends – this was possibly the last time I saw her sadly. She was a ray of light. When we sat there a large gentlemen hoved into view walking along the road with a long stride. This was Woody, we'd met before briefly. He was mostly blind, using tunnel vision in one eye to walk the Camino – he'd done it once before and had a tattoo to prove it. In my new found understanding of the human condition I admired this man's sheer bloody mindedness to succeed. This was a nice break – and then onwards – up over a hill then down along the road and over another hill to another village nestling in the mountainside. There were some ancient houses overlooking the way, Tudor style. Cross members of ancient timber leaned out as if to fall upon you. These were very old houses. Maybe 300 to 400 hundred years old. To Americans and Australians, I wonder if they realised that almost everything we were walking by, was older than their country? I'm sure they do, which is one of the reasons why they come back so often to Europe, where so many of them are spiritually, and genetically from.

Suddenly on one of the timbers, were two kittens looking down on us. Tiny new-borns – and there was one, on the ground and an angry mother puss was coming to pick it up. Why, then? When at that time, on that day, where we were looking for signifiers? After the villages we entered an area where the Camino suddenly went from steep to vertical. We were sliding down these stony paths made slippery by the passage of millions of pilgrims and at one point I had to clamber down the path as it was like a high broken wall of stone and I needed to be agile to get beyond it. I was a little ahead of Jim so I slowed up to give him a hand and to just be a support as it was tough going. At one point I could see the road and there was Woody marching along like a demon, cars swerving around him as he adopted a fuck you attitude to anyone or anything that wasn't a pilgrim. The route went through some smaller villages where even at this busy time of year, cafes were closed. There was another ten-foot section that was a jagged wall of stone, and you had to watch your footing to clamber down it. It was now very warm as the cloud had burnt away and it was hot, hard, sweaty work. In these situations, you look to your water because you can't seem to assuage your thirst when you're exerting, and the relentless sun is beating down. In due time the next village appeared lodged in the crevice of a valley, either side of a shallow mountain river. And there was the obligatory Roman bridge for us to cross. This was Molinaseca. There was a stunning church overlooking the town and I remember arriving on the bridge, grey -white in the sun, and I looked down to the river bank on the other side and there, under white sun shading canopies was the most beautiful bar I think I have ever seen. I pointed it out to Jim and I said 'Mate, we're going in there!' he agreed with alacrity. We ran into Woody again and helped him down the alley into the entrance and out on to the terrace. Within minutes we were sitting under one of the canopies with the coldest draught beers I have ever had. The bar owner, this beautiful man, just adopted us as his new sons and served us beer, and melon and serrano ham, and other delicacies and we just dived in.

Oh man, once again, I'm gone at the memory.

It was so perfect. I was so lucky. I am grateful to the Universe that we inhabit, for that moment. And as perfect as it was – I tell you, it got even better. I chatted to Woody, he had big Camino Tattoos from previous trips. He explained about his tunnel vision and how he coped using his phone, amazing. His attitude was just fabulous. We were all emotional. Poor Jim had been through one hell of a day and I could see it in his eyes. There was a quiet moment.

Then the tranquillity was ripped through by a woop from the bridge which was above us. There was this huge hairy smiling face, triumphant, delighted, victorious Huw! He fell into the bar with us, we shook hands, and we sat there drinking and eating in this magic place. Woody and I were talking, and I noticed Jim and Huw were getting emotional. Beth had sent Jim some pics of us at the Cruz and it had brought it back for him, and of course Huw had his moment to remember his nephew. I put my hand on Jim's shoulder, and we all shared a second or so of support. That defines the pilgrim for me. Strangers united. Immediate friends. Humanity being there for each other. I spoke to Huw, I said 'Huw I feel I have misjudged Alec,' I explained our conversation and how awful I felt. Huw smiled and said 'I'm warming to him too – you're right – we were wrong.' When you read this Alec, I'm sorry. You're now my friend and the Sonnet at the start of chapter 7 is for you. Thank you for showing me my failings through your openness and good-natured friendship.

Now, as I try and navigate my life, with all its loneliness and upheaval, I think of that day, that moment, where nothing else mattered. Sitting there as the water gently babbled by, the sun was kept at bay by crisp white cotton, and the beer, with ice floating in the glasses slipped down so easily. Plus, Jim craftily went and paid the bill too, his treat. Jim, thank you for doing that. I know it was your pleasure to do so. You're a lovely, generous man.

**Two Gents ready to drop – walking down from the Cruz de Ferro – me and Jim.**

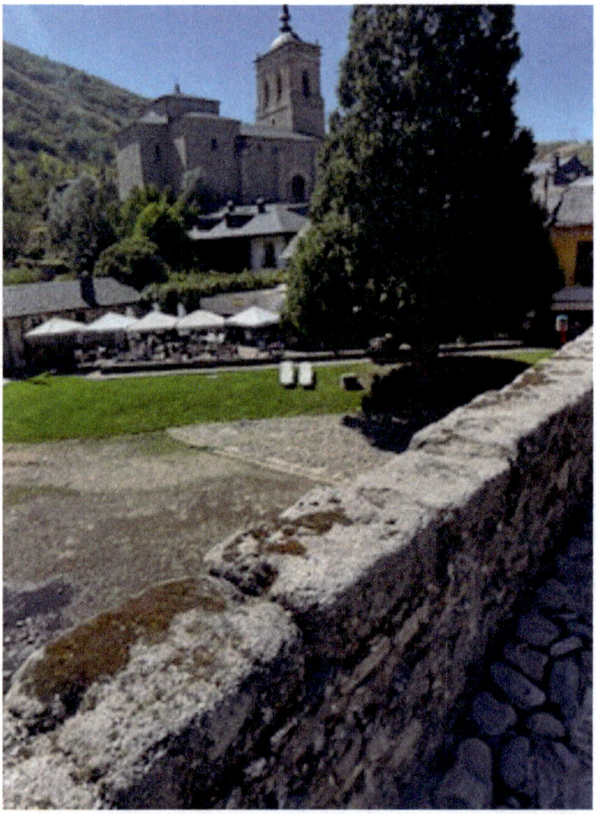

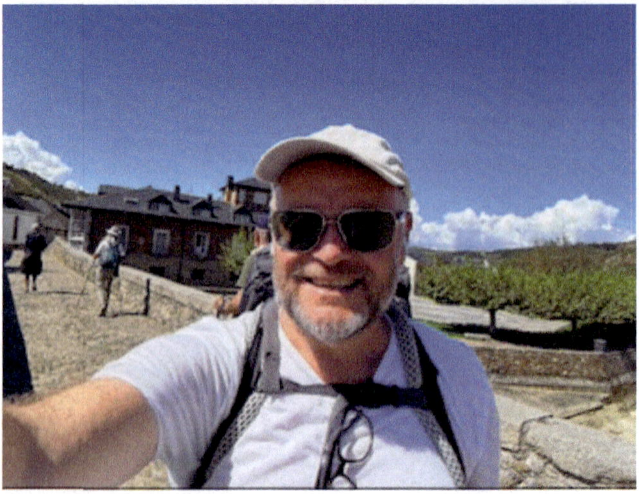

That bar in Molinaseca – oh! to be back there.

It was another 8km to Ponferrada, and Huw had practically ruptured himself catching us up so was staying in Molinaseca where I know he eventually shared again with Calamity, and stayed, by contrast to our bar owner who was amazing, with a hostel manager who was offensive. Huw said this guy wouldn't give you the steam off his shit, which is an enduring image.

Jim and I really didn't want to leave but Beth was waiting in Ponferrada and we thought, it was only another 8km so it shouldn't take too long. Sadly it really did. Ponferrada is another one of these towns built on a plateau, for defence I suppose. The route was a massive loop along roads that took you well away from the town before it looped back in. You could see the town right there, to your right, but every step seemed to take you further away. We laughed about it, but the emotion of the day meant we were pretty spent as we eventually crossed, yes you guessed it, another bridge and entered the town. I said I would see him later which I did. When we said goodbye we embraced. We both knew what a day we had been through. I'd do it again and again, any day.

There's a wonderful scene in Ingmar Bergman's film *'The Seventh Seal'* which is set in medieval Sweden. In the lightest scene in the film, the company, travelling players, the knight Antonius, and his servant, they all sit in the sun and drink fresh milk and eat strawberries. There is an atmosphere where they laugh and tell jokes, and sing songs, and there is an air of summer and peace amidst the terrible world, that is not far from them. The knight says, 'I shall remember this hour of peace, the strawberries, the bowl of milk, your faces in the dusk, I shall remember our words, and shall bear this memory between my hands, as carefully as a bowl of fresh milk, And this will be a sign, and a great sufficiency.' I know exactly what he means. These moments, so rare, once experienced, are always there to remind us of the urgency and beauty, and brilliance of life.

Ponferrada has an old Templar Castle which is used in Coelho's *The Pilgrimage*. I walked past it to my hotel. I had booked another, cheaper hotel just to have privacy after the nightmare of the loft in Foncebadon. It was a 26 km day, one way or another and we were spent. I found the hotel and fell on my private, double bed, then bathed and lay for bit listening to a guitarist play outside, again, why then? Music is such a validator.

I then went to get a drink, and sure enough there were Jim and Beth in the square, lovely to see them. I was smoking a bit, I enjoyed it after the day we'd had, with a cold beer. Bought some from a machine in a bar. In the square I ran into the gang – the Americans and older Matt plus Mike, a very small but perfectly formed chap, and Dawn and Alec. Alec had an amazing experience at the Cruz, where he had asked some picture takers to move and they had, and respectfully gave him some time. God knows what that was like for him, but he seemed lighter somehow. We were all smiling, laughing, as if our burdens had gone, disappeared somewhere. There weren't many restaurants open, either because it was the day of the week or because there had been a big fiesta on the previous few days and they were having a day off so we all agreed to go to a Pizzeria where we had beers, wine, and lovely pizza. This was also another great group and it included Rocky. She was another Australian and she was compelling. She asked you questions, and she was generous to a fault and warm and funny. Everyone loved her. Another new friend whom I would see more and more of over the coming days. For the second time that day the bill was paid for me. Mike was going early the next day and making it to Santiago in a few days and returning to the US for a family wedding, and as a treat he bought us dinner. How wonderfully kind. Thanks Mike.

My hotel wasn't that glam, but the bed was what I needed. I had a beer at the bar before bed, and I fell asleep clothed. Eventually I got in and slept. Dreamed the whole day through again.

The best thing about having a hotel room is being able to shower in the morning before walking. This is such a luxury. And then once again, no breakfast and out onto the Way. This exit from the town took you across roads and parks and past a great café where I got a pastry and coffee and there was Rocky – we chatted again. Then off we went towards Villafranca. The road out was very varied. You walked on tarmac for miles through the outskirts of Ponferrada, and this eventually took you to a larger town which you walked right through the high street. I saw older Matt zooming ahead, Beth and Jim in a café and various others all going at different speeds. Poor Jim had received further sad news from the US, and he was upset about losing yet another close friend. He was really going through it. This was hard going, and harder when you're carrying yet still more emotion. I hope the walking helped him throw off some of that.

There's no doubt that I was also moving faster these days, eating up the miles. I also had to phone to sort out a council tax issue at home and was on the phone for over an hour sorting this out. South African Jane passed me as I was berating a poor clerk at the council. In time this was all done and I entered a new and very vineyard framed area. This took you across a hillside of vines then through a couple of villages where literally nothing was open and thirst began to become a thing. The views back to Ponferrada were lovely and the sun soon baked you. The vineyards had a stunning white house set in the centre of them with views into the valley beyond, it was a total rural idle. Imagine living there, drinking the wine you're cultivating! The incline increased through a pass and suddenly you were up a steep way into the village. This brought you out at a café where beer and tortilla were taken. It was then a steep hill downward into the town and there in front of me was the Hostel I had booked in Villafranca. This was a stunning building with the friendliest man you ever met running it. He took me to a dorm – no bunks just comfy singles and I paid my meagre bill and asked to have the menu del dia later. He was the sort of guy who smiled and was always tapping you on the shoulder or arm to reassure you – more of this later. I checked in, went for my shower which was good, and then bought a beer and went and sat out on the terrace. The entire front of the hostel was in the sun making it feel like a very high-quality hotel. The girls were there and Elegant Cathy and South African Jane. We agreed to eat together later. Suddenly as we all sat there smoking and drinking in the sun, a huge number of giant sized, papier mache heads and bodies arrived. These were carried by children, and painted very brightly, and were carried into the courtyard and after a huge amount of sweets and hotdogs were eaten, they proceeded to do a kind of Morris or folk dance in front of us. This was a fiesta of some kind and subsequently after inhaling a million e-numbers and reconstituted meat they followed the 'puppets' down the hill to where bands were due to play in the square which was further into town. There were bag-pipe players – no thanks (I agree with the actor Matt Berry who says that bagpipes sound fucking terrible in any language!) and a drummer and a fiddle player, and there was a nice summer atmosphere about the place. Thinking about it, this was at the beginning of September and perhaps the children were having a last fiesta before going back to school? After the excitement we all spread across the terrace again and sipped our beers. I sat there with a lovely cold one, poured by the chap who touched my arm again, and as I relaxed in my sunglasses and lit a Chesterfield, I closed my eyes in the sun and allowed my body to suddenly sink into the chair, whilst one leg rested on another. Whenever I showered each day I would stretch my legs in the hope they wouldn't seize up and it is remarkable how the body adapts to constant effort. After a while it simply gets used to it and you feel fit enough to crack on. Today after a couple of beers and ciggies I was allowing my body to really go, to relax, and it felt like a summer holiday, still. As I breathed in the sweet tobacco smoke and allowed the aroma to gently spiral around my head, and then gently blew the chocolaty smoke out, I felt a presence to my left. Something was there. A presence was there, that I felt, next to me. I thought for a moment it was one of the grotesque and colourful heads left behind, but this was too small for that. I opened my eyes and looked to my left. 'Jesus!' It was Calamity. 'Blimey Jane, you frightened the life out of me – you okay?'

Why did I ask are you okay? I then got a 30 minute tirade about how she had been cut off by her bank and couldn't get money out. She'd been in Ponferrada in the bank that day accessing funds and refusing to leave until someone coughed up. There had been some mix up and she had spent days without much cash. She was smoking and looked exhausted. I'll say this for Jane, she was a tough bird and she wasn't going to give this up, so she fought until they gave her a few hundred euros which meant she could continue. Apparently, she'd spent the night with Huw in Molinaseca and then cracked on to Ponferrada where he was staying and she had walked on after the episode at the bank. I then realised that she had arrived after me and that there were spare beds in my dorm – oh my god she was sleeping next to me and Huw had warned me that her snoring was legendary!

Calamity had a reputation that she probably didn't deserve and I'm sorry that she had that effect on us. I offered to lend her money if she needed it. I had offered some to a British girl a few weeks before because I saw on the Camino Facebook page that she had lost her wallet, I don't mind lending – I trust people. But Calamity was okay – she asked for a couple of fags which I didn't mind and then she went off to shower etc. I sat with Elegant Cathy for a while and the girls were chatting to their Italian friends. Nicole and I had an absurd argument about who was the greater artist, Prince or Taylor Swift! Emmanuele, a bald chap with a deep dark beard was the unelected leader whom they all zoomed along with, trying to keep up – he only ever flew past me on the Way. We had a great chat about courgettes and how well they go with pasta and I agree. I've added courgette to all of my pasta sauces ever since! I've found out since that he was copping off with Kylie, who was 19 from the States – what a great holiday romance they were experiencing, no doubt. They were occasionally joined by another Italian who always looked and appeared to be stoned and I think he probably was. He was always very polite but looked like he was smashed to bits. I remember after Ledigos in the sun he blundered past me stinking of what I like to call a 'jazz cigarette' and then sat down very definitely at the side of the road – it takes all sorts.

Back in the hostel in Villafranca I could have gone for a wander, but it was such a nice terrace and in fact such a nice hostel I just didn't want to leave. So, we sat there drinking beers. As the evening wore on the girls popped to a river for a cold swim – good for them – and in time we sat together – the younglings on one table and me with the ladies on the other. That evening was so lovely, Sitting with Elegant Cathy and South African Jane, both Janes in fact, and other nice people and everyone chatting. The dinner took a while – beefsteak but it didn't matter. I made the point that the chap who was serving us – the guy from the hostel, was always touching my arm. Cathy was mortified that he hadn't touched her once! At one point he served me a drink and rubbed my forearm! This was hilarious. I think Jane got a touch too, and maybe Calamity did. At some point I think Cathy must have said something or given him one of her lovely smiles and he rubbed her shoulder. We cracked up. Thank god.

The girls on the other table got hammered too, and Brooke from Australia came up and was all cuddly and rubbing my arms and shoulders too – my god they were getting a workout today!

Some of the American girls went down to the square where they meet Alec and Dawn and Jim and Beth and danced to some live music, which by all accounts was a scream. I was very tired and a little tipsy from the wine and the beer. I eventually slid into bed only to be woken by a cacophony of snores – not just Calamity to be fair – my entire room was a choir of snorers. I pulled my pillow over my head and manage to drop off, no doubt adding to the snorer's harmony. Tomorrow would be another hard day's walking, and my final, big mountain.

**Chapter 9. Villafranca to Sarria**

Bob's Camino Playlist Song: Babe I'm gonna leave you by Led Zeppelin

*'Babe, babe, babe, babe, babe, babe, baby, oh baby*
*I wanna leave you,*
*I ain't joking woman,*
*I've got to ramble,*
*Oh yeah, baby, baby,*
*I will leave you*
*Really got to ramble*
*I can hear it calling me the way it used to do,*
*I can hear it calling me back home'*

**Sonnet 9: The Last Mountain**

We all dreaded the final, big mountain
Twenty K, then eight more straight upwards
Some would be waiting at a low village
For a comfy taxi up the steep hill
Others would weigh down a poor scrawny nag,
And expect it to drag them up the incline,
And I went on slowly, trusting the walk
The days before, prepping me for this climb,
Each stage had its long heat and mottled shade
Each bar dispensed beer and warm tortilla
And the view grew behind me at each step
Until it filled my vision forever.
The last mountain of this long and kind road
The last, whilst carrying a heavy load.

Now, you will remember my exchange with Mariel from Oviedo? So, here is where things start to get a bit interesting and I hope, entertaining. Unprompted from me, she gets back in touch after blowing me out at Leon, and asks where I might be in a few days' time. I suggest Sarria, which I know is a town of some size. She agrees and says she will drive down from Oviedo and meet me for lunch in a couple of days. Now, you can imagine the effect this had on me. I luckily still had a nice new t-shirt that I had bought in Burgos that I hadn't worn yet. I also worked out that if I went further in two day's time to Samos, I would get to Sarria early in time for lunch. It's amazing what motivates you.

So, when I left Villafranca I was up with the lark – actually the cyclists had all woken me in the early hours anyway, and Calamity telling someone to turn a light off. I managed to get my stuff together and leave in the dark. I was nervous about this day's walk. There was a long flattish route, and then it went sharply up to O Cebreiro, the final high mountain of the Camino before the lower hills of Galicia – and in fact at this point we were to pass into Galicia for the first time. The flat bit I wasn't bothered about but the flashbacks to the Pyrenees were still strong, and I was counting on getting a bed in the village at the top, which meant I had to get there in a reasonable time as it was a municipal hostel who didn't take advance bookings so, first come first served.

  The Way took me through Villafranca, some narrow streets of the main town and thence to a café on the outskirts where everyone had stopped for coffee and pastry. The harassed owners were doing their best to serve everyone but there was a group tour in there and they were rushed off their feet to say the least – I managed to get my meagre fair and sat for a bit before making my way out as the sun was coming up, out onto the roadside. Quite quickly I fell in step with two German ladies – one a little older – Joy, short dark hair and clearly a seasoned walker looking at her tan, and also Heidi who I had met before who was 19, blonde and fresh and very fast. We walked together and chatted for ages. The path took us along roadsides and motorways through high gorges, apparently there was a more picturesque route over the mountains but we couldn't see in the half-light where it started. Joy and I talked about children, she had a son, and also about the Camino. Heidi chatted for a while then sped off ahead – she really had thin little legs that worked like pistons. Incredible.

In time the gorges gave way to more villages and cafes. I stopped at one for more coffee and older Matt was there, possibly younger Matt and Lizzie and others. I was saying hello to people fairly constantly from now on until the end of the walk. Older Matt was the one who told me about Samos which is a loop that takes you off the main drag of the Camino and then winds down across country to a beautiful monastery. I didn't mind about that, but if I could make that walk the next day, about 30km, then I only had 10km to go to get into Sarria for my lunch 'date'. It was now well under 200km to get to Santiago. We had walked over 500 km from St Jean since the 19$^{th}$ August. It was now the 14$^{th}$ September. Near the villages were livestock like donkeys in fields and amazing goats hanging off the side of vertical cliffs. There wasn't much climbing for the first part of the day. The sun was high and it was very warm but not an oven. The Way led us through a verdant deep gorge that was stunningly beautiful. When I look at the pictures of this day, this was one of the most beautiful, one that grew steadily more so as the day went on, as was the next day to prove too, for different reasons. After the yellow dryness of the Meseta this countryside was a huge motivator. By midday I was still going pretty flat through the valley, taking pictures of the scenery, and loving the walk. Joy and Matt were passing me, chatting away, and I was enjoying feeling good, and also relieved that I had already despatched around 19 km that morning. Suddenly it went sharply up. There was a village where I stopped for a wee, and it was still not too hard, and then suddenly with no warning it went straight up. I took a picture of this turn in the path where what was a flat route suddenly changed and became a rocky, steep and hard climb. I leaned in and realised that I could do this. I just needed to keep a slow and steady pace and it would be alright. Much of the path was covered by trees so it was shaded, just steep and rocky. And relatively quickly I made my way up this incline. This went on, twisting and turning upwards for an hour. It was hard, but when I looked behind me, I couldn't complain, the view was so clear and beautiful. I kept wanting to stop to look back at it. I arrived at another village perched on the side of the mountain and there a café had tables looking at the view – a perfect place for the weary traveller to stop and have a beer and tortilla – no I wasn't sick of it yet – and see where I had come from. The kind café owner served me at the table and I asked him about his arm of tattoos as I was approaching Santiago and nervous about having my first one there. At this village there were a few small horses tied up under trees that you could book to sit on and take you the rest of the way up the mountain. I could see why it would be appealing especially if it was even hotter than today, but they looked exhausted, poor things.

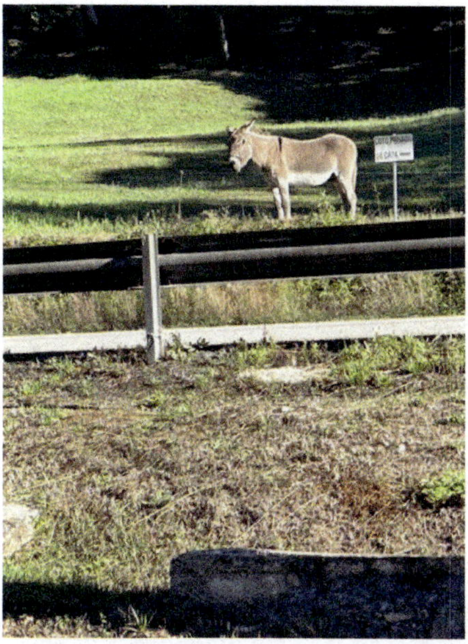

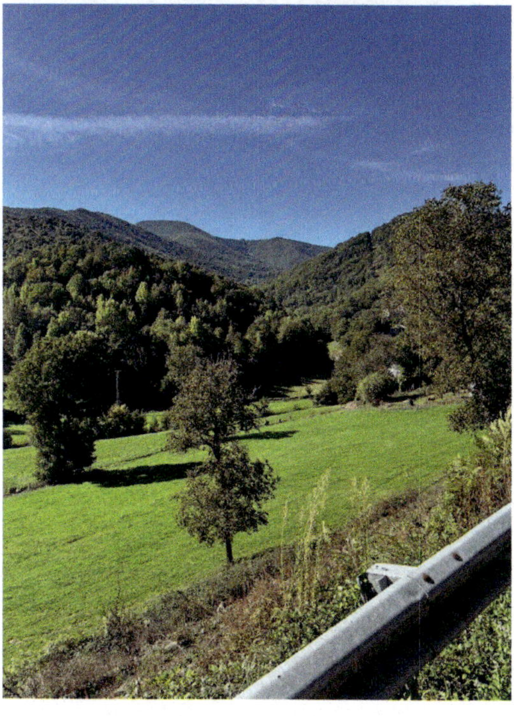

**The Walk Up O Cebriero**

From this point there was much less tree cover and you were walking in open sunlight on rough paths, up a steep incline. I decided to use my music and to talk to the sparse pilgrims to engage them and give myself some motivation. I spoke to some French ladies and Koreans, and everyone I met. I stopped when I could, loving the view, and in time, made it into the final village before the walk to the summit, where Matt and Joy were at the bar. It was a hostel too, and Jim, Beth and Huw were to stay there and walk up to the summit the next day. I was determined to do the last 4 or 5 steep kilometres to the summit. I enjoyed a large beer with Matt and Joy which hit the spot and made me pretty tipsy. I remember laughing a lot with them at the table, and then realising that if I didn't leave then, I wouldn't make it to the top at all.

I'm so lucky that I made that choice. The next day the weather changed and the same walk would have been far less remarkable. As it was, I walked up the hill, which was easier going than I thought, and as the view reached its widest expanse the beer gave me added energy to follow the contour of the mountain towards the summit. You realise you're nowhere near much up here. You feel very fortunate and I didn't feel too exhausted. I was enjoying it. The path leads along a series of treelines until it shifts and you cross into Galicia and a monument greets you. I was pleased to say goodbye to Castile et Leon and reach a region which didn't seem to be having a war with itself on every sign I saw. The mile markers on the Camino changed to Galicia style with very accurate kilometre measures to take us into Santiago – around 150 kilometres away. There was still a small distance to get to O Cebreiro village and there were statues on the side of the walls looking at the view. It was truly spectacular. I looked at that view for a long time. Once again, I was moved by how insignificant I felt seeing the rolling hilltops going back towards the Cruz de Ferro and Astorga and I considered the wonderful journey I had been through since Leon. The village had small 'hobbit' style houses, low stone homes with straw roofs on top. Some said they were Tolkien's inspiration for Hobbiton, but I wasn't sure about that. The mountain top was exposed but with the sun out it had a bracing feeling about it as you walked past the small church and into the village. I was looking for the hostel, and there she was in her beady hair, chatting on the phone, sitting on a wall, with the view silhouetting her, Marienma. She looked up at me and I raised a hand and thought about how she had told me she was unsure if she was finishing the Camino or not, all those days before in Estella. 'You made it this far then?' I said smiling – and left her too it. I knew my place and wouldn't encroach upon her anymore – if she wanted to be my friend then fine but I wouldn't push it. I went up to the lovely, purpose built and modern hostel, checked in, and immediately had a shower. I was really pleased with myself. I'd come a long way and scaled the final mountain in far better condition than I ever thought possible. I changed into another fresh t-shirt and made my way down to a local restaurant. I was very hungry and polished off three courses and a bottle of wine with no problem at all. There were all sorts of types hanging around, American chaps who looked like they had started at Leon, and a Spanish girl who was a stunner and insisted on wearing skin-tight leggings which set off her figure amazingly. I enjoyed my meal, texting friends and relaxing with a few fags after the long walk. This was at about 4.30pm, so it was really dinner. I then went for a walk around the village a ran into Alec and Dawn, and Calamity, South African Jane, and others. I had a few beers with Alec and Dawn. They were great company. We all knew we were in a stunning place. I think Beady Marienma walked by. I know Bonnie did. We were talking about property porn, where you can't stop looking at amazing low-cost properties abroad, online. At that point Bonnie breezed by and I said 'talking of porn, here's Bonnie!' she gave me a smirk and raised her finger 'fuck you Bobby!' – all well and good. It was great to sit, and drink and smoke. Maybe the altitude made us drunker. Younger Matt and Lizzie were there and we went into a little supermarket together that was stuck on the side of the mountain in such a way that you had to cross a narrow bridge to get into it. I bought some sweets to munch and some more fags, Camels I think.

As the evening wore on, I got a message from Huw and Jim and Beth who were back at the last village with older Matt. They would have loved the village I was in.

Then something happened that I didn't anticipate. It had been a clear day, and of course, we were at the top of a mountain, and the view in the other direction, the new direction towards Galicia was vast. There were few clouds and we were about to experience the most amazing sunset. Everyone flocked to the west facing side of the mountain and sat or stood, and watched.

My pictures, again, can't do this justice. The sun started to go quite quickly and the sky was ablaze with reds and golds and blues and greys and we bathed in its changes. Matt, Lizzie and I changed position to see as much of it as possible. Everyone was quiet. Everyone was lost in the beauty of watching our Earth turn, and our sun slowly closing the warmth on a fantastic day. We were like multicoloured ants scattered across the hillside, frozen as we took in the golden sight before us.

I was emotional of course. How could I not be? I believed that I did not deserve any moments of happiness like this. My god, it doesn't half show you what you are when you are face to face with the Earth in all its glory. And with the sunset the distant hills were changing colours, those hills we would soon be walking through, they were beckoning

us, and they looked so beautiful.

**That Sunset on O Cebreiro**

I thought about the people in my life whom I would love to have been there with me. All of them. Standing here with me, sharing this moment. Instead, I was with new friends and I was glad, but I missed to my very heart, every single person in my life, those closest to me that I wanted to share this with. The uniqueness of each sunset is like a gift.

The most amazing free gift. I kept saying in my brain, I am in the most beautiful place. I felt so diminished in the site of such beauty. And there was a sadness here. This was the last mountain. And this was the last real challenge. And this was the start of the home stretch. And there in the distance that I could not see, but which was surely there, was real life.

I didn't want it. I wasn't ready for it. It was going too quickly for my brain to cope with. My mind was no longer being supported and inhibited by anti-depressants so every emotion was raw and real and I felt it hit home very hard that evening. It felt like a wave of warm, hard tension was flowing through me. There was a sharpness in my breath and a stinging around my heart. My mind felt so happy to be there and yet so utterly alone and it cried out, silently, with pain that could never be expressed. I felt unloved. It felt so terrifying to be there, up so high looking at so much beauty and facing it without any feelings of love. O Cebreiro is just one place where I left a piece of myself. It will always be there. That sunset flowed through me and broke me once more on the road. The Camino has bits of me all along it, blood, sweat, and a few tears, and memories and connections to my past. Maybe here, I left behind a piece of me, and asked the Universe for something to replace it. Or perhaps, I was asking to give myself permission, to begin the search.

The next dawn I was exhausted. I was opposite a droning snorer all fucking night. The girl above me had buggered off hours before, clearly unable to cope with the loud bastard. I managed a few hours in between waking to this guy's horrendous snores. I think he affected Bonnie, Kylie and Emmanuele who were in the same dorm. I got my stuff as early as possible and was ready to go by about

6.45. But it was pouring with rain. The clouds had come in and enveloped the mountain and it was soaking. Everyone put if off for as long as possible, even Marienma I noticed, who normally left in the dark, but eventually there was no choice but to hit the road. So, wearing my trusty jeans again, and jumper and jacket and hat and hood I struck out through the trees this time heading down O Cebreiro. This was a gentle incline most of the way through trees and above brooks and when the trees were around you the rain wasn't too persistent. An hour later it has stopped and it was just very damp under foot. On this walk Paul was flitting about. He was a funny chap who tried to run everywhere. I don't think I ever saw him just walking. He was Canadian I think – possibly an American. He was making a documentary about the Camino and had a decent camera and a drone he occasionally sent up to film the pilgrims and the road. He was always trying to get ahead and so he sent his pack on (paying his 6 euros) and skipped along the way, always heading somewhere... can't wait to see the film, mate!

There were a couple of damp hills and I walked with Matt and Lizzie a bit. Older Matt had gone on ahead. He explained that he was going to walk faster and go beyond Santiago to Finisterre. Matt, who was ex US army, and Lizzie, were always relentlessly positive. He always gave me a hug when I saw him. Early in the walk, near Najera in Rioja he confessed he had been so worried watching me hobble along that he was delighted when I appeared one night in a bar and welcomed me like a lost pilgrim – which I was. He was talking about his retirement – I envied him that. I don't think I will ever be able to retire.

We stopped at a nice café for coffee then I moved on quickly, keen to get down to Triacastela and then on to

Samos, because my 'date' in Sarria was tomorrow. I cracked on, scaling another steep hill, then relentlessly down through the hills, those hills I'd seen from afar the night before, with the mountain diminishing in my wake. There were large statues of pilgrims now, along the way. Galicia seemed delighted to be the destination for so many roads to Santiago and it was celebrating that fact with giant pilgrims welcoming you. The walk down to Triacastela was uneventful as there were villages every couple of kilometres. At one I stopped and ate my first slice of almond cake – or Camino cake – sprinkled with icing sugar – delicious. The views became less mountainous and more rolling, and for a time I ran into Tricia again which was lovely. We were all on a mission to get to the next place. Almost everyone was staying in the town, I was hell bent on going the extra 9km to Samos.

Triacastela was rather an uninspiring place and there was a café on the hill as you entered. I had a beer then cracked on through the town. The first three kilometres beyond, on the Samos loop was roadside. Then suddenly you went off-piste and for the next seven you went across country through firstly, lovely small villages and then also you were led down ancient moss-covered pathways. I was alone for this entire stretch. It did not matter. It was green and rural and warm. The pathways were challenging but you truly felt you were walking in the footsteps of millions of pilgrims who had travelled this way, and made a point of stopping at the monastery in Samos. I knew it was a 30 km day, but then only 10 tomorrow! Plus a date! With a lovely woman! Oh this was going to be perfect! Having said that, I was aware that I hadn't given my clothes a good wash since Foncebadon so I made sure I was booked into a Albergue with washing facilities. The afternoon wore on and it got hotter, and my legs began to drag. My stick was essential for leaning and I was heavily drinking water. Some of the villages weren't much and there were no places to get a cold drink. This was about a nine-hour walking day with breaks and I staggered into Samos. The walk was lovely, but the extra distance after schlepping up the mountain the day before had exhausted me. The things you do? The walk in to the Albergue was quite long as the village stretched along another valley. I went past the Monastery which I am sure is great and is very large, old and impressive and you can imagine pilgrims lining up to stay there many years ago, but as you know I have very little interest in such things and I went to the Albergue where I had a nice double room to myself and a bathroom!! The lady running it agreed to do my washing and set to it whilst I went to a bar and drank the local cider which was recommended, called Maeloc which was cold and refreshing. I drank that with some cigarettes and went back for a nap. My washing was drying in the courtyard – poor woman having to handle the dirty stuff! – and I had a sleep because I was exhausted. In these quiet moments sitting in bars, alone, with no other pilgrims present, I was becoming far more comfortable. I was able to sit with my little notebook and work on poems and thoughts. I could call home and check on my boys and also just watch the world go by and count my blessings. As far as I could see the twenty odd kilometres from Triacastela to Sarria was a fairly straight walk along roads and I couldn't understand why everyone didn't take the Samos loop, especially as it was so beautiful. I eventually had an early dinner back at the bar which was good. I bought a leather thong style bracelet from the nice lady. I wandered back to the hostel and had a pretty good night's sleep in my double which felt very old fashioned but comfortable enough. I was probably averaging about 5 hours per night. It's not much, but sometimes when it's quiet and you're not surrounded by snorers it's good to get a bit more in and feel the body give in. The good news was that I was only 10km from Sarria which would take no more than a couple of hours so I was bound to be there by mid-morning which meant I had time for a shower before meeting Mariel, which I was excited about. Many of you reading this will sense that I am heading for a surprise or disappointment, and some will be unsurprised to hear that I'm getting both – but let's wait for the fun shall we?

The next morning I leapt out of bed and packed. Sadly, my clothes were nowhere near dry so I packed them into a plastic bag and would have to dry them later but at least some of it was clean. Then I donned my pack and was on the road by 8 o clock. The Way went out of Samos, on the road, along a river, and then took you up and above the river on a wooded path. It was a lovely fresh morning and the path was just like the day's before – mossy paths and mossy rock covered tunnels to walk up and through and beyond, and trees all around and small farms and tiny villages with tiny churches dotted long, and everywhere that little yellow arrow showing me the way to go. I was high above the river now hearing it flow by below and sometimes solo pilgrims would stop and listen to it – one man looked like he was going down to jump in. Good luck! I went through a couple of villages in locations above the river and eventually edged out onto the main road to the east of Sarria. There was a camping/lodge type place with a café in a field where I stopped and had coffee. I know South African Jane stopped there and slept in a lodge which I'm sure was fun. The coffee was okay, then on through the field back to the road that led down to the bridge at Sarria. Yes, another bridge – why the surprise?

The walk across meant that you then had to go up into the town and Sarria is a very high town. I went up a high number of steps and up a steep hill to my hostel. The owner, bless him, was having a baby and had left all of our keys in a box on the door trusting everyone to do the right thing. I loved that. I went in, found my room as his post-it said, and hey, I had it to myself – another 8 bed room and just me! I hung up all my clothes to dry on hangers in the window and on the window sill and then went to the bathroom to get ready. I showered and washed myself extensively and used the meagre after shave I had with me, and also dug out my best and cleanest t-shirt, bought specially. By now it was around 11am and we had arranged to meet for lunch at a restaurant that Mariel had found and booked. I thought it would be good to message her and just confirm I had made it to the town. I did so. A short period of time went by and the response arrived. 'Running a little late, we will be with you at 1.30-2pm'

Yes, there is a word there isn't there, that neither of us, dear reader, were expecting; 'we'.

It hit me, Christ what a fool. Of course! Of course! She has a boyfriend and her coming to see me was a kind act and nothing more, what the hell did I think was going to happen? That after a couple of zoom meetings and a few texts she was rushing down for 2 hours to jump into my arms? What a bloody idiot and I can hear the waves of laughter coming in my direction. Well, at least I was prepared. As I walked down the hill to the restaurant I guffawed with laughter – at least I had a good story now for the pilgrims. Oh well, hey ho.

I had time to wait so I had a beer opposite. Huw hadn't done the Samos loop so was looming down the road towards Sarria – I promised to meet him later. I drank my beer and waited patiently. Occasionally as the beer entered my blood stream, I would laugh at myself and considered the strange image we have of what we think we are. I imagined myself to be this windswept and interesting pilgrim but by god I was a heavily white-bearded, paunchy middle aged Englishman, and the very idea that this Columbian stunner would be in any way interested in me is utterly crazy. Again, the Camino teaches me a lesson. Or had it? Wasn't I still tilting at women?

In time I went across to the restaurant where there was a table reserved in a covered annex - very pleasant and cool, and I sat there waiting. Then they arrived. Mariel, looking lovely in a crop top, with her winning smile and beautifully styled hair, we kissed cheeks and then there he was, Rouven. Slim, about my age, dark, handsome, a CEO, nice chap. And we proceeded to have a very pleasant lunch – I didn't realise it was a menu del dia – only 12 euros each, so when I picked up the bill at the end I was hardly Mr Big Shot. During the meal we talked about our lives. She was investing in start-ups and he ran a soft drinks business selling healthy soft drinks across Spain. He looked pretty tired with it all but then they had just driven down here for 2 hours to see some mad fucking stranger. I must have made such a comical figure to them both, and I can only imagine the conversation going back. They were and are really nice people. We laughed about, and agreed on, many things. She's an amazing self-motivated businesswoman, who came from Columbia under her own steam and forged a successful career in Spain, and has an amazing career ahead of her. I am grateful to them for coming down to see me. It was a supreme act of kindness that I won't and cannot forget. The pendulum swings and time shows us that even when we think we have learned something, we haven't learned a thing. Maybe, finally, I will stop letting foolish thoughts command my actions.

They left after the pleasant lunch, and I strolled up the hill to the hostel where my clothes were drying and I napped, before walking down to the river for a snack with Huw. I knew he'd love the story and did, and we enjoyed a laugh at my misfortune, and my general stupidness when it came to women. It was good to see him, my double act partner on the road. He was feeling much better, the toe was on the mend and we sat in a café by the river watching the sun go down which wasn't nearly as good as watching it from the mountain. We were now only 5 days out from Santiago. This was a shock to both of us I think. Huw was trying to arrange for his daughter to come and meet him there from London, and was finding hotels ruinously expensive. I had booked mine already and my flight was arranged for 2 days after arriving there. This was crazy. We had been walking for over four weeks and were now approaching the end. I remember in the early days, thinking about what a wreck I would be when I walked into the square in front of the Cathedral of St James, and wept at the thought, and now it was nearly upon me. I've said it before, I did not want this to end so soon. It was ending. I was trying to slow it down to enjoy each bit, but then at the same time I didn't want to finish at a different time to my new family of pilgrims, now we were all in step. Even at this point I wasn't sure if Huw and I would finish together, or even if he would want to finish it with someone. It didn't matter, we were gearing up and each day we were completing the daily walks a little faster, which meant we could go further each day, and then we would finish far more quickly. We agreed that we would walk to Portomarin the next day. He didn't fancy the walk up the hill that eve so I went back up alone, ready to meet him as he passed my hostel in the morning.

When I got back up there everyone, the Americans, Alec and Dawn, Rocky, Bonnie, possibly young Matt and Lizzie, were in the bar near my hostel and I had to confess about my disastrous 'date' that they all knew about and found highly amusing. I didn't mind. It was another lesson. We sat in the square and there was a new American guy who sat with us and was inquisitive but bone shakingly dull. Sir, I have forgotten your name and I'm sorry to say this but you would bore the hind legs off a Galician Donkey. Yes, that's a judgement and I'm sorry for it. It's interesting I wonder if my new friends all thought I was a stupid fool when it came to women? Well, that judgement is spot on. My bed was calling and I left my friends around the table and went to my quiet room where I was looking forward to a lovely night's sleep which thankfully, was forthcoming. I squirmed a bit when I thought of the embarrassment that I'd been through at lunch. Oh, the stupid shame!

Sarria was a bigger town than you realised. There's a reason for that. If you can get yourself to Sarria and then walk the five days or so into Santiago it's just over 100 km and you can still have a certificate to show you've done it. So, lots of people arrive at Sarria for short pilgrimages. Especially in September. Especially the day that I was there.

**Mossy Walking, Samos**

**Chapter 10. Sarria to San Xulain**

Bob's Camino Playlist Song: Hard Headed Woman by Cat Stevens

*'I'm looking for a hard headed woman,
One who will make me feel so good,
And if I find my hard headed woman
I know my life will be as it should.
I'm looking for a hard headed woman
One who'll make me do my best
And if I find my hard headed woman
I know the rest of my life will be blessed...'*

**Sonnet 10: The Camino Double Act** *(for Huw)*

Aside from severe foot pain, we would smile,
Trying to survive this crazy challenge,
And we're suddenly friends, we just got on,
And shared this strange road through many stages,
You walked for a cause, I walked to escape,
We hung onto the high bunks in hostels,
We bore wind and heavy rain in the Meseta
We delighted in dramatizing the cast,
The people who watched pilgrims come and go.
The pilgrims who we made laugh, every day,
Calamity, Elegant Cathy, Jim,
The girls, the ladies, faces, embraces,
Thanks for the advice, when I was in need,
Like-minds gave both, someone on whom to lean.

Heresy. The Camino has a number of Facebook pages. There are pages for all routes, and specific routes, and you can join a few. I had joined one and this was because I had heard that a British girl had lost her wallet and this page had been a useful way to get the word out to fellow pilgrims. The posts though, are largely people completing their Camino whatever form it takes. Some of it is quite evangelical. To the point where it was slightly dangerous, to say anything, and I mean anything, that could be construed as negative about any single aspect of the Camino. As if it was a sacred journey that could not and should not be touched by human criticism. So, I am writing this next bit with a word of caution. Some pilgrims will, and did, struggle with the truth that my heretical view is about to explain.

    I went downstairs to check out, and there was the man who had just had a baby. He showed me a picture on his phone of the new-born boy, sorry but the name escapes me. I congratulated him and we spontaneously embraced. Nice way to start the day. Then I went out to the café opposite to wait for Huw and had a quick coffee and pastry. Eventually he appeared and we promptly got lost trying to get out of Sarria – apologies. When we got back on the right track we zoomed along the way, past one group, then another, and then we saw a school group, and another larger group of female Spanish friends in immaculate walking gear, and couples and families all BEGINNING their Caminos there, that day, from Sarria. The way became very busy indeed. So much so that at one point we were walking in front of a large group of kids who were playing deafening music as they all gently hopped on by. There were suddenly large groups of cyclists coming along and getting in the way, there were more people on the road which meant if it narrowed and they were slower than you then everyone behind had to slow and the thing became, comparatively, a bit of a farce. Huw and I were incredulous, not that we had any particular right to peace and tranquillity but compared to what we were used to this felt like it was taking the fucking piss. Heresy. I could see it from the teachers point of view. First week back and you take the kids, whilst the weather is still okay, on a five-day trip which starts the term off well and they can do a project all about it. Plus, you avoid teaching for a few days. Brilliant idea. Nice for the kids too I suppose, but again, for us, the real pilgrims from St Jean I'm sorry to say this stuck in the throat a bit as we struggled to get along at our usual pace and also how long we had to queue for food in the now, very crowded cafes. This was a bit of a shock. We stopped in one café, everyone we knew practically was there and the queue was stretching out the door. We had never seen this extreme of commercialisation before and we feared it would be like this all the way into Santiago. We saw Calamity a few times and she looked pretty miffed at this sudden business. At one point Huw lost his temper and stormed through a bunch of kids bellowing something in his actorish way and they parted like the red sea. And off he went up this roadside exclaiming something about the 'fucking crowds! Of fucking amateurs!' probably in Welsh. Careful, because for some this is real Camino Heresy.

The walk to Portomarin was lovely I recall, very green and fresh, but by god it was busier than we had experienced. The other worry that suddenly appeared was this, up until now Huw and I would wait till about lunchtime, call a hostel on the list, and reserve a 'cama' (bed). Now, whenever we called a hostel in Portomarin it was 'completo'. The busy way was bad enough, this insecurity about a bed was now shaking us to our very core. I don't think that we felt we had a right to a bed, but this was so unprecedented. It was only 18km to Portomarin, and we passed through many small villages. The locals are aware of this sudden increase in pilgrims and are ready to take advantage of it in every café, and some bright spark had dressed up in some weird local get up and was playing a set of bag pipes to help us along the way (still sounding fucking awful) plus this guy was playing no discernible tune that I could hear, just going up and down the scales. The cafes were damned busy and we passed several before we saw one that was just being vacated by a large group of school children and was now quiet, so in we went.

Every day we'd enjoyed a Spanish omelette for lunch with a beer, and most of them were much of a muchness. There was no real difference between those in Navarra, Rioja, Castile or Leon and we hadn't thought much about it, and just assumed the Spanish had at least unified around one style of tortilla that most enjoyed. In this café, the owner, a rotund and smiling lady, had made her own tortilla and this was twice the size of any we'd encountered. Not only was it massive, it was moist, clearly made with many eggs, and the cooked but still gooey yolks were dripping down the sides. We had two large slices and made sure she understood that this was the best we'd had on the whole Camino. I think we was pleased, but then she probably knew that already.

Once in a while a tiny village would appear and we would go through and hit a huge smelly dung pile which, when the wind was in the wrong direction would be offensive. I saw one lady's washing hung up in one farmyard, the smell of the yard was noxious from the road, so god knows how bad her clothes were going to smell.

On this day in a hamlet, was another Albergue dispensing free beers (for a donativo) and we had one so we could use their facilities. It was in a very old courtyard with colourful designs on the wall. The gate was a large wooden affair, very old, that reminded me of the gate a Hougoumont, the chateau at the battlefield of Waterloo in Belgium (1815).

Eventually the ground fell away from the countryside, towards a wide river, spanned by a very long bridge that went straight across to the town. We had made mistakes almost booking rooms or beds that were miles away from this place because when a town is full, the App just suggests places 'near' and doesn't understand that you're walking and can't drive on somewhere. The bridge was very high up, and the river below was stunning, with some ancient structures visible above the water. Clearly, it had been a busy Porto at some point. When we got to the other side we walked right through the town calling at every place we could including hotels, to find any rooms or beds. Everywhere was 'completo'. Huw decided to use charm. He went into a small Pensione run by a middle-aged lady and asked for two beds. She clearly explained she was full, and his pained reaction meant she took immediate sympathy and got on the phone and found us a twin room in a hotel just up the road. It was 100 Euros between us, including breakfast, we said 'fuck it', beggars can't be choosers and went for it. We wandered along, it was a few hundred yards away. We checked in, showered and then went back to the main drag for some drinks and to meet the crew. The main hostel had an annexe but this was locked shut and no one had any idea when it would open. We sat there for hours with Rocky and others, whilst the queue grew. I noticed Marienma had managed to get into the main hostel. It's funny that whenever we saw each other now we just ignored the other's presence or just smiled. Calamity and many others were all sitting outside this locked door and were waiting for someone to open it up, this seemed ludicrous, plus you couldn't reserve a bed so if they filled up you were buggered. We had a few beers which took the edge off, but everyone, from the St Jean starters, were shocked at just how busy the Camino had become and there was concern that it would be like this all the way into Santiago. So, everyone was consulting their apps trying to work out where would be the quieter places where beds would be more easily found and where we could experience some tranquillity. I did not meet anyone who thought the added walkers were fine, or fun. We ate some pizza, and Huw went off for a nap. I sat with some of the younglings and it was pleasant enough. I'm pretty sure Jim and Beth had an extra day in Sarria so they would remain a day behind us as we got into Santiago. There was always the option to slow down, rebook my flight home, and I was also thinking about going to Porto on a bus after the pilgrimage for a few days, but I really wasn't sure about anything. However, my head was about to get turned for the final time on the Camino. That evening we ate in a restaurant that was run by a miserable looking Maître d who served a barely serviceable Menu del dia. The prices were definitely rising as we approached Santiago. Another heresy.

We finished and got out of there and wandered back to our very busy hotel. Huw and I were sharing a room which was fine – we'd done it before but even so we both wanted some privacy. He went up and I went out onto the terrace at the back to have a ciggie and to make some phone calls.

So, what I haven't explained so far, is that for the previous few days the Scandi artist and I had been having regular text-based contact. All very positive and 'twinkly' and I had sent one that day making a radical suggestion that we move on to an actual vocal conversation. She thought this was an exciting innovation and we were due to speak that night. I sat outside enjoying a drink and a fag and chatted to a lovely, positive, funny person who was just great. This rocked me, I must say. I'd run into her a few weeks before and thought, not a chance. Here she was talking to me and chatting, and we were getting to know each other. She was a therapist anyway and totally understood the therapeutic benefits of doing a walk like the Camino. She had done something similar a few years before. She was unmarried. She was blonde, beautiful and seemed to like me? WTF? Something was bound to ruin it, but then maybe the universe was moving in its special way to bring people together in the right place and at the right time. That sounds like there's divine intervention, surely? Or is it just luck?

    That night, I'm sorry, Huw snored like a docker. My sleep was disturbed. I woke needing the loo and couldn't expose him to that so I crept out to the downstairs loos where I could go in peace. In the morning, we woke early and after some prep we went down for a wonderful included breakfast that as pilgrims, we really weren't used to. The breakfast room was full of wealthy, clean and well-dressed pilgrims. They had clearly joined yesterday in Sarria and they had had a very low temperature introduction to the Camino. One chap was in 'pressed' walking trousers and his walking shoes, such as they were, looked brand new and didn't have a spec on them. Huw and I considered ourselves the pros, struggling on in our meagre wardrobe, whilst these amateurs strolled along dressed like kings. Heresy. Who cares? Let them wear what they want. I know.

We had worked out that the next stop, Palas de Rei, about 25km on, would be rammed with pilgrims, much like Portomarin, so we reckoned if we went 3km further to San Xulian we would get a bed, and we booked it in advance. We had to walk back across the town which was busy at 8am. Not nearly as busy as the Camino suddenly became. What had been an influx of a few hundred the day before became an influx of thousands that morning. We crossed another bridge to get out of town and there was a great deal of road following on this route. I saw one path following a road up a hill. There was a mass of people picking their way up it. There were no gaps, just a continual movement of people. More large groups, schools and student groups, families, music blaring, like organised civilisation had descended on this quiet place. At yet another packed café we queued for a stamp (you needed 2 stamps per day now on your Compostela) and a coffee and when we sat down I went onto the Facebook group and wrote something like 'The Camino is very different after Sarria, be warned its harder to find accommodation and there are big groups joining here making the path very busy. I really hope it's not like this all the way to Santiago'. Heresy. Many people immediately agreed – 'yes it's like this all the way in, try not to let it ruin it for you.' Or 'Yes I was very disappointed by this – there's nothing you can do.' So lots of people felt like I did. Then I got a load of criticism, 'imagine walking all that way and being that intolerant' – something like that. This has nothing to do with the criticism. It's Christian and Camino fanatics who refuse to accept any words of criticism of their beloved way.

I think if I were being that intolerant I would have just got on a bus. I was just stating facts. It *is* a bit of a shock to be sharing the experience with a mass, not just a few, a mass of newcomers, some of whom are there for a school trip and can only make it bearable for themselves by playing loud music. It *is* galling after weeks of routine to have that blown apart by mass uncertainty and it is a bit rich for Galicia, to gently increase the costs of things like meals and hotels from this point. Everyone has the right to make some money, but Huw was royally screwed for his hotel room in Santiago, as I was actually, and it's unnecessary. Without the Camino, and its many variants across northern Spain, what other reasons would there be to visit? It's lovely but it wouldn't be on your usual list of destinations I think. The commercialisation which had increased from Astorga was now everywhere. Heresy.

You're walking along, listening to your music or an audio book, or walking up a hill leaning on your stick and enjoying the scenery, because it is very lovely. And you hope that everyone is enjoying it too. You're wishing that this wasn't ending any time soon either. Then you feel a presence and 40 people march past you, and music is blaring from a large battery-operated machine from someone carrying it at the back. Why they think this will enhance their walk I have no idea. Maybe it's the only way they can persuade them to do it? And I have to listen to that from before they get to me, whilst they walk past me, and for a minute or so after they've passed. Purists will say 'oh let them do that if they want to, what harm does it do?'. Good question. Except that the Camino is a personal experience and this is anything but, now. And these are my final days and I want to squeeze out every piece of therapeutic goodness I can, and I don't want to feel resentment towards the crowds – I don't – but I do feel a little fucked off by it. At one point we were in a café and one of the younger chaps came in, who knew us, German I think – and he made a point of saying very loudly 'Ah yes here are some pilgrims!' pointing at us. We burst out laughing. You think that somethings have been preserved for posterity and that the Camino is one of them. So why tell people they can have a Compostela completion certificate from 100km out? Why not make it 200 or 300? I know it's cynical but it's about money, of course it is. And now some stretches look like a queue at Disneyworld, not that I've ever been to one. Heresy. How can you be so selfish? If I was alone in this theory I would be inclined to agree, but I am really not. After Sarria, the Camino is more money focused and that is a damned shame, and some, not all, but certainly some of the magic, is lost. Heresy. If I am not careful, I will wake up with a horse's head in my bed.

    Eventually the path went across country again and became steep which slowed some down and the groups naturally had to split and break as people walked at different speeds – this improved things a little. There was a lovely feeling walking over heathland with no sound of traffic and you could feel yourself breathe again. There were loads of villages now, with strange storage buildings in each garden or yard. Huw and I sometimes walked together, sometimes split. It was a good partnership. Sometimes we didn't speak. We didn't need too. One newcomer that morning was walking in a black Fred Perry t shirt and jeans and trainers. He was very tall and it looked a bit unusual. Later there was a cloudburst and the poor guy was sitting in a café later with steam rising from his soaked, skin-tight jeans, and had water dripping down his face. You would never have walked from further out – say Leon, without the proper gear, and now we had 'day traders' thinking it was akin to a stroll along a river on a Sunday afternoon. Oh Bobby, you damned heretic. My correspondence with the Scandi artist was increasing with flirtatiousness since our conversation and this was very positive. I was now considering going straight home as planned so I could see her. Oh, you romantic fool, man! I think it was this day that I had a 2-hr long conversation with K. It was a gentle, pleasant, positive chat. We laughed a little, and I thought she sounded more positive than she had for ages. I was feeling forgiving and sympathetic. When I suggested we ring off she didn't want to. She kept wanting to keep talking. We talked about all sorts of things. I'm sorry to say she never asked me anything much about my trip, I had to volunteer most of it. I got her laughing about the accommodation and some of the hardships. I know that despite everything, here was a soul who needed some help to change. Many of you will be shouting 'get out of it man!!' but I honestly felt detached enough to look at this situation objectively. It's hard for anyone to make definite choices when the heart is involved. Well, it's hard for me anyway.

So, after 20 plus kilometres or so, we finally came down the hill into Palas de Rei. Huw had cleverly arranged with Elegant Cathy to meet us for lunch when we bowled in and there she was outside a bar waiting for us. We all sat and had a drink and a bite and I think South African Jane joined us too. These were formidable and organised women who had nearly completed their Caminos and they'd travelled from other continents to be here. It was amazing how quickly we had become mates. The bar was full of builders and the other bars were full of parties of pilgrims, and it was going to be a busy town and there wasn't much of a town to be busy in. After saying goodbye to the ladies it was a 3km scoot uphill to San Xulian which was a tiny village with a hostel in the centre. We checked in to a small dorm and confirmed we'd be eating there that night. The way was cobbled and the hostel had some shady areas to relax in. I was sitting in a shady nook having a fag and writing a poem, when Beady Marienma walked by with some other bloke. She had no choice but to say hello to me, which she did, and off she went again. She was moving pretty fast these day but we were keeping in tandem. I then went across to a larger area where others were sitting and I tried to write some poetry. An American chap was arguing with a German I think, about religion and the stilted conversation became wearing in the extreme 'but if you look at scripture' he kept on saying, as if that was the answer for everything which for him it probably was. The European voice of reason was being beaten down and I could hear him conceding for a quiet life. When the evangelist realised he'd been a bit a zealot and tried to backtrack, it was too late.

The village had a couple of good sized Horreo's on display, these are granarys or storage huts for produce that can be kept rodent free for long periods, outside. They're all the way along the Camino in Galicia and I've never seen them anywhere else. We naturally joked that they were used for keeping slaves, servants or other hidden family members in. Some were very elaborate, probably where the farmer kept his mistress? That evening we had a nice menu del dia with wine for not much money. We had to agree to pay our bill by card the next day which was fine. We sat at our table, Huw and I, and we must have been quite a sight. There was a mother and daughter in our room as well as some blokes. It was a narrow stone room and the snore echos were going to be massive. There were two loos with showers that were very nice, except there were large holes, high in the walls that went through into the dorm at the top of the walls. You could bear the shower water running when people were in there and when someone went to drop a depth charge you could hear everything! I went in the middle of the night. It was also quite warm in the sleeping room so I kicked everything off and just lay on the mattress. Thank god that this was all before the bed bug epidemic that engulfed Europe later in the Autumn. The next morning the mother and daughter were fast asleep and we didn't want to wake them so we had to lift our stuff out and dress in the vestibule. It was an early start again and as I had coffee and pastry I watched as our friends who had left from Palas de Rei, walked by the open door, and many waved. In the night I had a missed call from K, I didn't know why.

We were three days from Santiago and the end. It was close now, and the milestones recorded distances were going down quickly. We were about 50 km away, which meant two medium days, then one short day to get into the city. I started to get agitated because this was too good to finish, and I didn't want to go home, I just wanted to keep walking and I didn't want to say goodbye to these people who had come into my life and now all meant something to me. That morning in San Xulian, I sat drinking my café con leche as the sun started to appear, and realised that not only were the days going quickly, I was going much more quickly. My fitness had reached a point, which seems crazy, where the distances weren't enough. I was so used to 20km per day that I could have feasibly made it into Santiago in two days but we'd worked it out, Arzua, then Lavacolla which is actually near the Santiago Airport, and then that left only ten kilometres for the final morning. Thankfully there were some beautiful walks still to go.

**The Camino Double Act – me and Huw.**

A Horreo in case you were wondering.

## Chapter 11. San Xulain to Santiago

Bob's Camino Playlist Song: Better Man by Paolo Nutini

*'And you'll either love me, or you'll hate me*
*Cause I can see you got no time for the in between,*
*But the reflection in your eyes*
*Gonna look so much better'*

## Sonnet 11: Leaving it on the road

I was moved when I walked onto the square
But not as much as I had expected
It was early, but already busy
I felt detached, tired and disconnected
I saw Cathy in white, visibly moved
And we hugged in warm congratulation
And then we were off to the stamp office
Celebration, and some cold morning beers
I returned to the square later, it rained
And I watched the crowd, pilgrims and poses
And searched for the emotion I had planned
It was not far away, lurking inside.
I realised that the Way had worked hard
Taking my pain, leaving it on the road.

K had called me in the middle of the night to say that she had decided to go away for an extended trip. It was her choice and I am glad she made it. This also meant that whenever I went home I wouldn't be able to see her, which was also a good thing. I had tried to move on somewhat and this would improve my chances of continuing this, and hopefully help her too. It did.

We ran into Rocky this morning and went through some beautiful villages like Casanova – and it was very green and rustic all around us. Galicia is a lot like Ireland or Southern England, or probably, Newfoundland. Galicia is by far the rainiest Spanish province and most days there was a small amount of rain. It was now much cooler as we were in late September. Some days the mornings, like this one, were chillier and I wish I'd brought more than one pair of trousers and shorts. Thankfully the vigorous walking kept you warm. I remember that day very clearly, we started in mist, and we loved the Celtic feel of it. It was beautiful yet familiar. It was less commercial and not too busy. Perhaps some of the fair-weather walkers were leaving it until later or were giving up?

I had been on this journey for 5 weeks. This is the longest time I had taken off for many decades and in real terms it had flown by. It was coming to its close and I felt almost that each footstep was a goodbye. The Camino still had many surprises, emotions and painful departures and new journeys ahead of us. I wonder now, if I had been more conscious whether I would have slowed down to elongate the experience, but I could not do that because of the community. Once you're ensconced in a group of people then part of you wanted to finish it with them. I still wasn't sure if Huw actually *wanted* to finish with me and we had both agreed that it was fine for us to finish separately. I was in two minds as well. There were lots of small villages on today's route which followed a shallow river and went mostly through trees and the pathways were not road focused, which was a relief, or indeed, too busy and there were plenty of moments of peace on the cobbled and rocky pathway. I reflected on the changing path beneath me, like life, it had many types. Smooth, flat, rocky, muddy, slippery, mossy, tarmac, or vertical, or smooth stone worn down by a million pilgrims all heading the same way.

The Way is a real thing. I don't mean the solidness of the path. It is almost as though there is a 500-mile tunnel that you walk along and within it is everything you need, people, food, water, beds, the path, the mental challenge, the physical etc. And there is nothing else beyond, not whilst you are on it. You know there is a world out there with war and famine and pain, and people that love and hate you, but whilst you're there you are spared that and you exist, I suppose, quite selfishly. You care deeply about what you are doing, the people you meet and you hope, and I really hoped, that the experience was working on my brain and improving me as a person. The App which helps you along and which we used avidly to calculate distances and the heights of mountains in the early days, we barely looked at now because the distances were so easy to calculate. The milestones were down to sub 60 km, we almost didn't want to look at them, it was going so quickly. Plus, there seemed to be more and more of them, almost labouring the point that we were nearly there. The milestones in Castile had mostly been specific distances to the nearest kilometre and these ones were exact 63.702 km and there were often 3 or 4 posts to a kilometre. There were villages of course, with statues (loads of Pilgrim statues everywhere) and cafes and Huw and I took some pics as we were running out of time now for memorable pictures. Because we were so close there was no need to rush. We had our beds booked so nothing to worry about there, we just settled in for the last few kilometres.

**Octopi**

Halfway along was a small town called Melide. We approached from the south and this brought us in towards the high street. There was a large bar on the corner, and they were frying up fresh octopi. This is a Galician speciality. The man cooking them had a look on his face that seemed to say, 'look at my fucking octopuses!!' as he chopped them up and fried them in oil and seasoning. Huw and I immediately went in, it was 10.30 in the morning after all, and had a large pile of octopus between us washed down with beer. It was delicious. This is another golden moment. Everyone, pretty much, who was walking that day, went into that shop and ate octopus – perfect marketing – just stick it on a corner and start cooking, next to hungry people who haven't had much for breakfast – and clean up. It took a little bit of time to get out of that town and then it became very tree covered with lovely wide pathways going through countryside. We split at that point for some reason knowing we would meet up in a little bit, which we did after 30 minutes or so. The sun was high in the sky and we walked down through woods towards a famous brook. The stream flowed over rocks and the sun shone through the leaves and made the inside of the wood shine with life. There were immense stones that were lined up as a rocky pontoon across the stream. This is quite a famous crossing point and many a pilgrim's picture is taken here, and we sure enough took short films of each other as we crossed. The stones were about five feet long, and about two or three feet above the bed of the flowing stream. The top was smoothed and worn down by the feet of a million pilgrims and we had just added to them. The countryside was funnelling the Camino into one simple direction – we were thirty kilometres or so outside Santiago. It would have been possible to get in a cab for 30 euros and get there. It was also funnelling our minds because we were looking for opportunities to take pictures to make more memories. The path to Arzua had many villages, and stream-side walks through shady trees, and small stalls at the roadside selling souvenirs. At one, I bought some simple string bracelets with earthenware symbols, shells, fish, and a heart for the artist. I was aware that I hadn't bought much in the way of presents for the family or anyone else, but also realised that there would be piles of souvenirs in Santiago itself.

It was on this day that Huw convinced me to stop smoking. He used an approach I had never heard before and it was very strong. He asked me to imagine the life that an American was leading, spending money he had earnt from creating an advertising campaign that many years ago, had persuaded me to buy a packet of fags. This is a good one! I hated the thought that my occasional habit was funding someone's lifestyle! Plus, it wasn't doing me any good. So, I stubbed out my last ciggie and I have not bought any more, much.

As we approached Arzua, we had to risk our lives crossing a busy road. By now it was a very hot day and the sweat was dripping down our backs. As luck would have it, a café was here, just on the outskirts. We bought beers and then we joined a multinational group of pilgrims who were all sitting with feet dangling in a freezing cold water-feature. We sat there sipping our beers and feeling the icy water cleanse and freshen our feet and then the chilled blood was rushing round our body's, cooling us off. This was a magic idea – South African Jane was there and we chatted with her and just relaxed. Smelly Christian was also there, well, at least his feet would be less smelly, and some Korean ladies and gents. Bonnie went by and some of the younger American girls. This was a real piece of heaven.

**Smelly Christian, South African Jane, Huw and Me – feet in the feature!**

In time we made our way through the town to the Albergue. This was a modern affair with no bunks and 6 or so beds to a room. I wasn't sharing with Huw this time but with some ladies of all nationalities. The hostel had a kitchen and Bonnie and Kylie went to buy cheap pizzas to cook for dinner rather than eat out. We, rather guiltily, went for a sit-down menu with Tricia and the others. We drank wine and I have a lovely picture of me and Huw with

Tricia, with the backdrop of the open country we had recently walked across. I remember not being too tired. These 18km days were now not a problem. Tomorrow was the last full day of walking and then it was the final bit into Santiago. Poor Huw was struggling a bit with his foot and was planning to walk some, but not all of it the next day as he didn't want to be crippled when we got there and his daughter arrived. Everyone was planning something. Elegant Cathy and most of the girls, were planning a few nights in Santiago and then doing the additional three day walk to Finisterre (the end of the Earth). Huw was having a few days and would bus it out to Finisterre, and other friends like Jim and Beth and Alec and Dawn would arrive the day after us. As for me, my return flight was booked for three days' time. The thought of it filled me with sadness. But every time I tried to slow the walk, it somehow moved more quickly.

My conversations with the artist had moved up a notch, so I was excited about that, and I wanted to see my boys again. Engage with life and work again? No thanks. If I could have done, at that point, I would have turned round and walked back again, at least as far as Astorga or maybe Leon, and go again, it had been so brilliant, but what was that? Just stretching out the inevitable. That dinner was a lovely evening. Tricia is a real power for good in the world. A genuinely lovely person with no side at all. It gives you faith in the human species to meet someone like that. I wonder if she, and the others, remember the days and evenings as I did, or whether they only keep hold of certain aspects or snippets of conversation? Whereas I am cursed to remember so many things. She talked about wanting to 'make out' with someone before it was all over because by all accounts Kylie and Emmanuele were an item, as were Bonnie and Nico (I was delighted to hear this) and she hadn't managed to cop off with anyone yet. It's so funny, isn't it? We all want the same thing in the end. I would have loved to cop off with just about anyone, but I was now realising that to be looking for it, like I had been, meant I was never going to find it. Whereas if I let it find me, then it eventually would. Tricia talked about an apartment they had rented in Santiago and did I want to 'dib in' and stay with them, it was tempting but I thought, like an old fogie, let them have their youthful time! And anyway, I had booked a hotel and I was looking forward to some privacy.

**Me, Lovely Tricia and Huw in Arzua**

The fact that the next day was the last full one, was on my mInd. I think it was about 24km, and I was ready for it. At the same time, sitting there in that restaurant with my friends, feeling nostalgic for what we had just been through I certainly believed that this final walk would be an emotional end to the 500 miles we had begun 5 weeks before.

I slept well and left a little later than Huw – he was laughing because he was taking it easy that day. When I left it was still a little dark, and I met Cathy on the Way a little through the village. I would miss Huw on the road today, but at the same time we both wanted a bit of time to ourselves.

You may remember that when I flew into Bilbao, I went to the barbers and had a short haircut. Similarly, I had trimmed my beard the day before and had no intention of cutting it at all before coming home. So now I had longer, springy hair, and a white, fairly full beard, longer than I had ever had before. Five week's growth. I had entirely got used to it and in fact was growing rather fond of it. I had hoped that the 5 weeks in sun, wind and rain, would have sculpted my face a little, and although I had lost some weight, about a stone, my eyes were puffy from lack of sleep, and I looked older, maybe more careworn. I definitely looked like I had done something with my life. I had hoped to look like a Mediterranean type but I looked like a knackered Norwegian fisherman! Still, if it hadn't changed me physically much, the walk had proved my organisational skills were okay. My bag, I had carried the whole way, never sending it on when it would have been so easy to do so. The underpants, t-shirts shorts and jeans, and my trusty jacket and jumper had served me really well. My boots, despite the blisters, were now my friends, seeing me through hundreds of miles of hostile, flat and rocky territory. When I look at the forums now, the Camino groups where no heresy is allowed, I see people wondering about these things, the basics. I just want to ring them all and say, just turn up, you'll be fine! And when some say – I can only do 4 days, which shall I do? I should be more forgiving and recommend Astorga to O Cebreiro, but I want to say, just do the lot! Why limit yourself? But that's not kind enough is it. I'm pleased they want to do it at all, and I want them to have the full experience – as many of my friends did, whilst they were still young enough, in my case just about young enough, to appreciate it and benefit from it.

That final day of walking, I was about 37km outside of Santiago, about 23 miles. The next morning I would only be six miles outside the city. In fact, I would be nearer the city than the airport. A couple of things happened that day that made it memorable. It was quite damp in the morning, and as I went through a village I took a wrong turn. I approached a stream and there were two geese. They were near a ford in the stream and were clearly very protective of it. Maybe it was my wooden stick tapping on the road, or maybe my red jacket, who knows, but these bastards went for me. They started flapping their huge wings and moving towards my legs. I did a feint with my stick hoping to scare them off, but they came straight at me. These weren't elegant Canadian geese, or white, swan like creatures, these were two big grey geese with orange beaks. I dodged aside as the lead one went for my leg and thought they'd give up after that. I turned round and found they'd circled – on their feet by the way – and were now chasing me along the path. I laughed out loud and told them exactly what to do. They pursued me for another twenty metres of so before spitting finally and stopping. Maybe they were protecting eggs, maybe they were just bad-tempered Spanish geese!

**Fuckers**

    The woods as you approached Santiago are full of Eucalyptus trees which are a bluey green and give off a certain scent. Huw takes the piss about my obsession with greenery and moss, and I understand that, but I suppose it's the prevailing colour that stays with you.

After Arzua there is a sequence of villages with open cafes. Along the way today I saw all my friends at various points. I noticed some lovely modern, purpose-built hostels which would have been nice to try. Depending on your level of fitness, you could easily be at one of these closer villages. Many would stop for their last night in O Pedrouzo before the walk into the city, but we had wanted to maximise our time on the day we arrived so had worked out that Lavacolla was the best bet.

There were even more stalls and souvenir places along this route although apart from a few roadside places most of it was rural. It was a good feeling to be moving along quite quickly on this day, probably at my peak of fitness for many a year. I was listening to my playlist which had been added too many times over the previous five weeks, and I had added an old favourite – 'Promised you a Miracle' by Simple Minds. I pretended my staff was a bass and 'slapbassed' it along the road at times, looking like a funky middle-aged chicken.

There was a road to cross at O Pedrouzo and rather than go into the town I had a Tortilla in a café on the outskirts, Tricia and some others were there and we chatted.

I reluctantly left that café, as this was the final pull into Lavacolla which meant walking around the airport.

Then an odd thing happened that I still can't quite explain. At one or two villages on, there was another bridge, and next to it a nice Albergue with a café. I needed a wee so I went in and bought a drink. Not long after Tricia did the same thing. At the time before going into the loo, I propped my stick against a wall. When I came out I stood outside for a bit, and then walked on and left it there. There was a steepish hill though the village and then back onto a rural hill heading upwards. About 2km on I realised, and then I was in a real quandary. Do I go back for it? Or leave it? It only cost 10 Euros and when I got to Santiago, I would never be able to take it onto a plane without paying four or five times its value, plus it had never really been mine anyway, it had simply replaced one someone else had taken. So, I texted Huw on the off chance he was coming through there – he wasn't – and then continued as I had begun the walk, sans stick. It had served me well, but I was about 15 km away from the end now and I think I was fit enough to see my way through without it. In the end, a thing is just a thing, and only we create fictional feelings in our brains, that the thing has created, or that it holds within itself. The stick was not missing me at that point, I am sure.

The eucalyptus trees led us through more mossy (sorry Huw) and very green paths. There was a large drystone wall, very old, covered in ivy (there's a new one for you) and again, you imagine the millions who had passed that wall over the preceding centuries. Then the path ascends through more woods until in front of you is the runway of the airport. You can see planes taxiing and there is a booth there selling refreshments – you could walk round into the terminal if you were that desperate. You then walk along the runway and bare left round the end of the airport and down the other side of the runway until you reach a stone monument carved by the bridge. It is a shell covered, carved decoration and the word emblazoned across the middle is 'Santiago'. I am now in the environs of the city of Santiago De Compostela which is only a few kilometres away. It's gone from over 800 in St Jean, five weeks before to less than twenty, and those are being walked within the city limits. It was still another seven km or so from here into Lavacolla. And from here we discovered a new spectacle, pilgrims who had already been to Santiago and were walking back towards the airport or had arrived there from another route and were doing the same – staying a few km from the airport and walking into it. I admired their commitment, but knew I would be getting a cab to get my flight. Moving away from the airport was a village with a route that took you around the church for no apparent reason and the cafes were closed which was a blow, then on across flat routes towards Lavacolla. This is a long village with quite a few Albergue and ours was in a converted factory at the far end. I was in good fettle as I marched through this town to the final hostel. This was a great choice, a modern building specially built with all mod cons and little sleeping pods with curtains and lights and phone chargers and seating areas – very impressive for 13 euros I must say. I checked in and then went over to a café where Tricia, Nicole, Rocky and others were enjoying a sit down, and we drank a couple of beers. Huw arrived not long after, he'd taken a bus for the final bit because of his foot, and we all agreed to go to the café across the way later. I then annoyed Tricia by getting to the hostel washing machine before her – I needed clean clothes for Santiago, but thankfully the washing cycles were short. She called me 'Bobby you little bugger' which is a term that never sits well in an American's mouth I find! Apologies Tricia.

After an average steak and chips dinner that night I was sitting at the table with Huw and Rocky. She is amazing. She is becoming the Director of a charity clearing landmines in former war zones and she was doing this walk, and other experiences, before her job began. What a great thing to do. We talked for a long time about that and had more beers. She liked a drink, Rocky, and always had to be restrained from buying them because she was so generous. Also, I looked at us that night and we were all tired. In every sense we were coming to the end. Huw and I were still unsure if we would end the trip together, which was actually fine. On the map, it wasn't very far, just 10km to the centre. Much of that would be through the modern city around the old town.

When we made it back to the hostel I chatted to a couple who had just walked the Portuguese route and were on their way to the airport – they thought I was doing the same until I explained, no I had come from St Jean. This was something they would have liked to do but could not take the time – I felt very privileged once again. All my stuff was ready for the morning. We all wanted to leave around 7.30 to get into the city early because we had heard that the queues for certificates at the pilgrim's office were long, as some 3,000 pilgrims each day finish their walked at this time of year, and we wanted a full day to celebrate and relax.

I slept fitfully on that bunk, excited, I think. I rose and some pilgrims had left already. There was no sign of Huw and we texted. He was back at the café we'd eaten at, the previous evening. I went over to him and he was waiting for it to open so he could get a stamp, as you needed two stamps per day and he had forgotten the night before. We agreed I should go ahead and I would see him there. It was very dark and there was a very odd circuitous route out of the village. The path went down towards a stream and there was a road bridge that crossed it but a wooden pedestrian bridge took you on a right angle over it and then back to where you would have been had you followed the road bridge. Then you went uphill through a residential village area, and eventually passed some large companies or factories that were bringing people in to work on buses. We had vaguely said that we would see the girls at Monte del Gozo – a view point where you could see the cathedral, but they were well ahead by now. I tramped on through the darkness and as the sun came up I was in a series of roads that took me through suburbs. I was motoring along, I thought, and when I arrived at the Monte (it was an incline) I realised that the monument was 600 metres off to the left. At that point I was joined by Huw – so if I was going fast he must have flown to catch me up. This felt right to me, and we crossed the park together and arrived on a hillock, certainly not a Monte, where two vast statues of pilgrims were raising their arms in awe at the sight of the cathedral. Here we stood and had pictures – so we could see it now, there in the distance, in the cool light of the morning, and it didn't look that far at all. The statues are dressed in monks habits and they carry long staffs with gourds of water and they are Christian Pilgrims so what they saw is so much more than we see – we see the end of something and some sense of achievement and they see salvation, the forgiveness of sins. Indeed, Monte Del Gozo means Mount of Joy, so there would have been a religious ecstasy at getting to this point, I am sure. Huw and I were relieved and also a little melancholic.

We crossed a big open-air amphitheatre to get back on the road, and then we were into Santiago proper, over bridges, roundabouts, past signs and cafes, and what looked like an entirely modern town at this point. Here's the strange irony, the nearer we got to the cathedral, it seemed we had further to go – as if that last three or four kilometres was really another ten. We didn't say too much. Huw was incredulous that it was taking so long, probably another hour of walking, all told. We were both puffing, imagining this last straight would take us there, but even then it took us to a long pedestrianised run up towards the cathedral. Huw walked a little ahead of me and I let him take the lead. He was doing this for very serious reasons, and he was dealing with all that too.

As for me, I was a little detached. I had dreamt of this for weeks. I had in some ways dreaded this moment, believing I would not be up to it. It had been a hot morning with no coffee or food, but even so, I was walking into this place not really feeling it, I thought, to the extent that I should. Suddenly the architecture changes, and you sense you are close to the cathedral. You can hear it, sense it, and as you walk towards a stair well you hear the bag pipes – again – playing a tuneless, and for me a pointless melody to pipe you into the square.

I was sure, for weeks, that walking into the square, each step, would be agony and that I would be inconsolable with grief. As it happened, Huw went on into the square ahead, and I entered to no fanfare, merely the light of the damp morning in that massive space where for centuries millions have walked before me and celebrated their arrival at the burial place of St James, the Apostle of Christ. I walked gently onto the square. Huw and I may have had a hug, I can't recall, my mind was whirling, and wondering why I wasn't a broken specimen. I looked at the Cathedral, and once again the architects of the medieval period had played a blinder. It's beautiful, a place inspired by faith to create a feeling for the faithful. It was still quite early, but a few were already having their pictures taken. The girls texted to say they were down getting their certificates at the office and that the queues weren't too bad. I stood for a while and let my mind try and make sense of this from my own perspective. I couldn't find it.

It took someone else's emotion to affect me. I saw Elegant Cathy, standing in her white top, visibly moved, and she had travelled alone on this road. I went up and tapped her on the shoulder and we had a very long hug. A hug to die for. Cathy, I hope it meant as much to you. You're a very special lady and you really helped me that morning. I felt some of my own tears on my face. We congratulated each other. My achievement seemed so much less compared to others. I did not feel the gut-wrenching emotion I expected. After a few pictures of our own we all sauntered down to the office where, after registering online, we were in and out in five minutes with two certificates. Huw needn't have worried about the extra stamp he had waited for, as they barely looked at the Compostela passports we showed them, and we were given a certificate with our Latinised name on, a strange gimmick – I am Robertum Morrell – and another confirming we had completed the pilgrimage. This was at 10.14am. By 10.24 we were in a bar restraining Rocky from buying more drinks, and clinking beers and tortillas which were lovely but a much higher price than on the Way. We had more pictures. We enjoyed some beers. We had made it and our walking journey, for some of us, was over.

**Monte Del Gozo (previous page) – Santiago in the distance.**

**WIth dear Huw**

In Santiago – taken by Elegant Cathy after a hug to die for.

**The Certificate**

**Early Beers.**

**Chapter 12. Santiago to Home.**
Bob's Camino Playlist Song: Promised You a Miracle by Simple Minds

*'I promised you a miracle,*
*Belief is a beauty thing*
*Promises, Promises*
*As golden days break wondering'*

**Sonnet 12: The Camino Dinner**

I was the oldest there by a long way,
Each hemisphere was there and we all knew,
That we had succeeded and won the race,
With ourselves, and that this group was unique.
Some flew along the Way, others strolled
Some snored, some craved love, wanted a hug,
The pasta delighted and the wine flowed
The speeches touched us, like tea in a mug.
I studied the faces, so much pure youth,
So much potential with wonderful hearts,
Faces will fade, some are hard engraved,
Through gratitude for their companionship.
There will never be a repeat of this,
Raising my glass, a moment of pure bliss.


It did feel quite odd not to have to walk any further. There

was much talk of when others would be arriving and also

of where we were all staying. Huw was meeting his

daughter later that day. The girls were going to their

respective places and I made my way to my small and modern hotel. I showered and changed into clean clothes and had a short rest. Then, of course, I had to go back to the square. Huw and I had arranged to meet later for our tattoos which I had arranged with Andrew in a place called Studio 20, about a 15 minute walk away.

At about 2.30pm I went into the Cathedral and, as you can't place your palm on the old stone anymore due to wear and tear, I touched a random stone column of the cathedral. I also lit a candle for those in my family who would have appreciated me doing that, and I took in this beautiful monument to someone's God. I didn't go and see the relic or hug the saint (yes you can do both) because it had no interest for me. I did walk out, back onto the square and sat in the corner, watching the people come and go.

Where was it? I thought. Where is that heartbroken

emotion you've been storing up all the way along, just for today? And yes, there it was. I could feel it there, somewhere inside. But it was reluctant to come out, or even let me know it existed. After some time, I concluded that what had happened was simple, the emotions around my own failures, mistakes, self-loathing and my own narcissistic tendencies had been mostly left behind, on the road. Those 500 miles had stamped much of it from me and as such, I had entered Santiago emotionally lighter than when I had arrived at St Jean. I liked that thought very much.

    I thought of my family, my boys and my wife whom I missed terribly, my mother who despairs of me, my sister who has to make do with a very part-time brother, and an ex-lover whom I knew would find stability and happiness without me. I thought of the friends who may or may not want to hear about this journey, of the friends I had made on this journey who had been extraordinary, and I thought of the uncertainty of my future. One thing I was certain of, was that whilst I live, this would not be my only pilgrimage.

I walked into the old town in search of a restaurant. I went past Beady Marienma who was sitting with some pilgrims and we acknowledged each other's presence, no more. I eventually had a burger and a beer at a restaurant and bought a few additional souvenirs for family and friends. Then I made my way across town to the tattooist. The studio was in a modern bit of town and we were early so I met up with Huw and we had a coffee, then went across to Studio 20 where Andrew was waiting. I had seen my preferred shell design on his web site a few months before, so I knew what I was having on my shoulder – a modern, illustrated version of a shell. The Shell I had followed for 500 miles. It wasn't too painful and was over in ten minutes. Stung a bit but was by no means the agony some had said it would be. Huw was next with his small red cross of St James – I remember him sitting there looking up at me whilst he was having it done, with a look on his face like he as having a pedicure.

We paid the man, then we bought moisturiser from the chemist and off we went for another beer to celebrate. For both of us it was our first tattoo, and we were both pleased that this was the occasion. That evening Huw was spending with some other pilgrims and his daughter, and I was due to meet the girls at their apartment. Bonnie had texted me saying 'bring wine' which I was very happy to do. I bought a few bottles from a supermarket and then went back to the hotel to rest up again before the evening, I suddenly felt very tired.

**Ouch!**

**The Dinner – Kylie has her back to me, to her right is lovely Nicole. Tricia in green, Bonnie in blue.**

There was good news, I was meeting with the artist for a date on the day I got back in the evening. I had something to look forward too. This was the Friday evening, and on Sunday afternoon I would be back at home. I didn't immediately tell everyone at home I was finished. I wanted to let it sink in first. And it was odd that this 26 litre bag had been my entire life for 36 days. Why did I need a whole house full of stuff? I was now measuring out my clean clothes, the next wash would be at home.

That evening I used my maps app to guide me to an apartment in one of the main drags, not too far from the Cathedral. When I arrived I pressed the buzzer and waited for a while – no answer – tried again, still nothing so I called Tricia and she came and got me. The apartment was on the first floor of an ancient building overlooking a street with balconies hanging over. It was very large, 4 bedrooms, with 2 reception rooms and big kitchen. Here Emmanuelle, someone I wish I had got to know better, was cooking a simple pasta and meat dish with mushrooms. Everyone was necking wine and some were dancing and there was a student, end of term vibe about the place. There were some more Italians I didn't know, a Norwegian chap who I had seen but never met, two more American chaps and the usual crew of Tricia, Bonnie, Nicole and Nico. Rocky was arriving later. There was a new American girl there with Paul, the documentary maker, and also Heidi the younger German girl I had met after Villafranca. I was, by far, the oldest person there so I felt very honoured to be invited. The Italians served up the pasta and we all got some, and wine was sloshed around. There was a long table we were all seated at, and I was at one end. I had been thinking about making a speech, and then I was trumped by the Norwegian Guy who stood up and gave a short, clipped and impactful speech congratulating everyone. We ate for a while and then I stood up. I said; 'Thank you for inviting me here tonight, it's wonderful to be with you all. I look around this table and we are here from every corner of the globe, this is truly a melting pot of humanity. Some of you I know quite well, some not so well, and one or two, I don't want to say goodbye to. (I caught Tricia's eye here) It's wonderful that we are all here together, because the Camino has brought us together. After that first day, which was so hard, I wasn't sure I could do this, and here we are. I don't know what your personal reasons are for doing this crazy walk, but I sincerely hope that as you sit here, you feel that you have at least found something, of what you were looking for. I know I have. So, congratulations to us all, and Bon Camino.'

We toasted and then we talked about the walk, where we were all going next. Bonnie was wearing a very loose silk dress with nothing on underneath. I know this because she kept falling out of it. She was pissed and emotional. The American girl with Paul came up to me and said she was moved by my speech. She then did a strange thing and tried to touch my heart but ended up on the wrong side and touched me above my right lung? She was probably pissed, too. Thankfully this wasn't the last time I would see them all. On this night, Nico said to me 'Bobby, you've completely changed on this walk… you're like a different person.' I found this very moving, by god, I hoped so. Mind you, what sort of a twat had he thought I was at the beginning? Rocky arrived and we sat together feeling quite parental, looking at them all get increasingly drunk. Tricia had her heart set on copping off with an older Italian chap, and sure enough she did! Good for you! After a while Rocky and I left them to it. As we left the building Nico and Bonnie were leaning over the balcony having ciggies in the night air. We bade them a goodnight and I said 'don't do anything I wouldn't do' which gave then plenty of scope. We wandered back and said goodnight on a street corner. We'd see each other tomorrow, my last full day. I was pretty pissed myself, after the wine, and very tired after this long day. I slept heavily.

The next and final day was started late. I lay in because I was winding down. I then spent time organising my clothes and packing as much as I could – a cab was taking me to the airport at 6 the next morning, so I wanted to make it as easy as possible. I went out into the Santiago world and that morning I met Matt and Lizzie and we had drinks in a bar. They had been real friends to me when my feet were falling off and I was glad to be able to see them. At this point I saw Beady Marienma. 'Fuck it' I thought, 'I'll say something' so I stood and said 'Congratulations – you made it.' And she gave me a hug. A hug of forgiveness? Certainly, of goodbye. We had mirrored each other along this road and I was sad I'd blown it, because she was really lovely, but I was glad we had ended well. It was a satisfying circle to close. Matt and Lizzie were going back to a life of fun with their families and I envied them when Matt was talking of retirement – he must have had significant Army service behind him to be able to retire on a pension – he looked younger than me.

One thing I had to be back in the square for was Jim and Beth's arrival. This coincided with Alec and Dawn's arrival and also Brooke from Oz, Calamity Jane, Alisha and Richard and several more of the usual suspects.

Huw and I met up there and we hung around waiting for everyone to turn up. His daughter had been very delayed on her flight and was sleeping it off. I think it was at this point I saw Alec and Dawn. He was very emotional, as was she, I think. I wandered over with my arms open to embrace. Dawn saw me first and moved towards me, Alec then saw me and shouted 'Bobby!' and leapt towards me. As he did so, he punched his arms into the air, and one hand, which was holding his iPhone, smacked Dawn in the face! We all embraced but she was in quite a lot of pain. It was clearly an accident but probably not what she was expecting. I congratulated Calamity and everyone including all the girls from the night before posed for a group shot.

**Calamity, Bonnie, Nicole, Me, Kylie, Brooke, don't know x2, Rocky, Tricia, Dawn, Richard, - ground - Alisha, Alec.**

There was a lovely atmosphere as the sun was out and this busy day in front of the cathedral was interrupted by a visit by the Spanish Prime Minister, who did a red carpet walkabout – of all the things! If only I'd realised it was him I could have had a word about my Camino feelings about the general commercialisation, probably best I didn't.

Then Jim and Beth walked over and Jim was very moved to be there. I hadn't seen him since Ponferrada so it was great to reconnect. After more pictures we went with Cathy and the rest down to the same bar as the day before and we had beers. When I look at the photo, I see Huw pointing, Elegant Cathy just looking so happy and Beth looking relieved, Jim totally beaming with his eyes sparkling, and Alec and Dawn chatting to Rocky in the background, and me, in my jeans and red anorak – I am so lucky to have met these people. I had no idea who I would meet, but these are connections that I cherish, because we shared so much. All of these people helped me through.

**Huw, Elegant Cathy, Beth, Dawn looking away, Alec (obscuring Rocky) Me and Jim.**

That afternoon after seeing everyone, I decided to pop into some shops and buy some more trinkets for friends and family, and then make my way down to the hotel for a final spruce up before the evening. I wasn't sure that I was going to go to a mass at the Cathedral. In the film, The Way, they watch the Butafumeiro, a silver incense holder, being thrown around, and it's all very impressive, but I wasn't sure if it was for me. In the end I decided to go and I'm glad I did. The Cathedral was packed with people and we all had to stand at the back to watch, luckily it was only a 40 minute service. It was all in Spanish and Latin and I couldn't pray, I couldn't go and take the bread and wine or receive a blessing. I already felt blessed for having arrived there with my friends. The priests threw the Butafmeiro around and the big ball sailed overhead and showered us with its rich scent. Then we were sent on our way. Later, my friend Ann's daughter, Katie, who knows about these things, said that anyone who completes a pilgrimage and attends the mass at the end of it, is absolved of all their sins. I didn't know this at the time.

**Butafmeiro**

After the mass I walked down onto the square as the sun set and took some final selfies, the last in daylight. I then went for dinner with Huw and his daughter Rebecca, Jim and Beth and Elegant Cathy. We sat there together and ate, the service was slow, and we reminisced about our Camino's. I have some nice pictures of us all in that restaurant. Cathy was going on to Finisterre the next morning. Huw and Rebecca were getting the bus out to it which sounded very sensible. I was on a hot date the next night back in England. After a nice meal, and not too much drink, in time we came to say our goodbyes. It was hugs all round. It was very hard to say it, especially to Huw, my new and dearest pilgrim friend, someone I had spent many happy days with on my Camino. He's a truly good man, with the softest heart under his gruff exterior. I gave him a tiny stone pilgrim to put on his desk. I won the Camino lottery that evening in Belorado.

**Me, Elegant Cathy and Beth**

As I left, I had one more appointment to make. Tricia had sent me an address and I walked through the old town streets for ten minutes, and there they all were with Rocky, in a bar. I had my last beer of the Camino with them and we all talked excitedly. Tricia was delighted to have 'made out' with the Italian gent, and everyone else was smiling because they, like Cathy, were walking on in the morning to Finisterre. Eventually, I thought, let's not make this hard, so I started to say my goodbyes. Bless her, Rocky called me Saint Bobby as we hugged and she still does. Bonnie gave me a hug and big smacker. I love that girl. It was hugs from Kylie and from Nicole whom I would soon see again in London, and hand-shakes with the guys, including Paul (who had copped off with the girl who put her arm on my chest the night before) and hugs from Dawn and Alec and we vowed to meet again in England. And then. Then came the hardest one. My little friend Tricia. She was in tears and so was I and she didn't want to say goodbye and neither did I. I wept. I do now. She was more important to me that I had realised. She was a constant positive. I'll always be grateful for her friendship. Thank you, darling Tricia. I hope you find your permanent 'make out' partner soon.

I walked down from the old town for a final time past the cathedral, this place we had all spent so much time and effort to get to. It looked spectacular in the moonlight and I took some final shots of this unforgettable place. Then I made my way back to the hotel for a deep sleep.

**The Cathedral of Santiago De Compostela**

At dawn the taxi came and twenty minutes later I was at the airport. I checked in, and my flight was delayed. I didn't mind too much. By the entrance to the departure lounge there was a big bin full of discarded staffs and sticks from the walk, which is where my poor stick would have ended up! I had an extended breakfast and worked on my poems and my memories and thought about the journey. There was a Spanish girl sitting waiting near me who had a shell tattoo on her wrist. I asked if she had just completed the Camino, but no, it was from the year before. The flight to London was two hours. I dozed for much of it. Landing around lunchtime. When I had left England in August it has been roasting hot and there had been a heatwave whilst I was away. Now, it was decidedly cooler. The train from the airport took me to London, where I changed for a train to Tonbridge, and then after a wait, to Tunbridge Wells. I retraced my exact steps from 39 days before, from the station across the road, and up over the Common. As I crossed, slowly, heading towards my little cottage, a man stopped me and asked where I had come from. What are the chances of that? A stranger. I said, 'I've just walked the Camino De Santiago in Spain.' He said 'Wow, that's amazing, congratulations – you look like you've been somewhere'.

    I turned into my road, walked through the trees, and there was my cottage. I entered and it was not quite as I had left it. My boys had used it as a base for a few weeks and there was stuff everywhere. I lowered my poor pack to the floor and placed my tiny stone pilgrim on my desk. I opened the door to the garden and heard the familiar toot toot from the nearby steam railway. I put on some washing and showered. I put on different clothes for the evening, and thankfully, my car started first time. I drove for forty minutes down to the coast. The sun was still up and it felt a little odd but good to be home. The run to the coast was easy, and I parked in a square in site of the sea. It was a little windy. I walked down to the seaside bar, and there, with her back to me was a blonde lady in a denim jacket. For the second time that week I tapped someone on the shoulder, and she turned with a beaming smile, and welcomed me home. You will be very pleased to hear that we had wonderful evening. Drinks, followed by dinner, and then snogs on a street corner! Not bad at all for a first date!

That night I went home, and the end of that long day, was the end of my Camino de Santiago.

**Afterword.**

All of the pilgrims from my Camino have remained in touch through several WhatsApp groups. I have seen Nicole and Alec in London a couple of times, and we did a walk recently in my new town, Lewes in East Sussex. Huw and I have met up too, in Soho, and the last time in Brighton, when he was filming, which was just great. Jim messages me, and I have sent him the excerpt about our day walking together after the Cruz de Ferro. Beth tells me she is still wearing the bracelet I got her, so sweet. Tricia and Bonnie keep in touch and I count myself very lucky to know them. Older Matt found love on the Camino and now divides his time between Vermont and Montreal. Paul, the documentary maker met another girl the night after the one at the party, amazingly, and I think they're now engaged.

I'm sorry to say that three weeks after my return, what started out as a promising relationship with the lovely artist, sadly, came to nothing. You will be pleased to hear that though I was sad about this, I was okay with it, so maybe I'm finally changing a little. I am trying harder not to judge people and trying to be kinder in general, and most of the time I succeed.

I loved my Camino, for all my complaints. I aim to do another as soon as I am able. I hope you all decide to make a pilgrimage too. There are shorter routes from Porto or you can do the longer Norte route along the coast, or walk up from Andalucía. The other one I like the look of is the Via Francigena that goes from Switzerland down to Rome. Better get some new boots. Bon Camino!

    The Nurseries, Lewes, East Sussex. February 2024

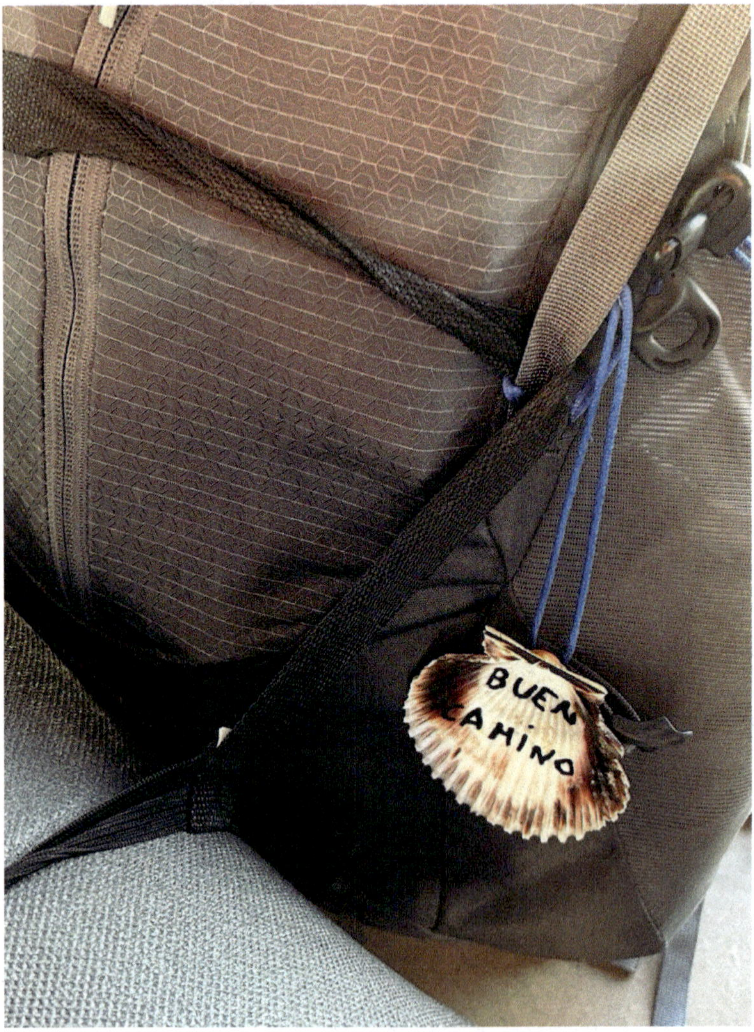
BUEN
CAMINO

Printed in Dunstable, United Kingdom